Body
Toxic

Body

Toxic

An

Environmental

Memoir

Susanne Antonetta

COUNTERPOINT
WASHINGTON, D.C.

Library of Congress Cataloging-in-Publication Data
Antonetta, Susanne, 1956-
Body toxic : an environmental memoir / by Susanne Antonetta.
p. cm.
ISBN 1-58243-116-7 (alk. paper)
1. Antonetta, Susanne, 1956- .—Health. 2. Environmentally induced
diseases—Patients—Pine Barrens—Biography. 3. Hazardous waste
sites—Health aspects—Pine Barrens.   I. Title.
RA1197.52 .A55 A3 2001
615'.902'09749—dc21   00-065868

FIRST PRINTING

Jacket and text design by David Bullen

Printed in the United States of America on acid-free paper that meets the
American National Standards Institute z39-48 Standard.

COUNTERPOINT
P.O. Box 65793
Washington, D.C. 20035-5793

Counterpoint is a member of the Perseus Books Group

10 9 8 7 6 5 4 3 2 1

Grateful acknowledgment is made to the following periodicals in which
several chapters of this work, in altered form, originally appeared: *Manoa,
American Literary Review, Gulf Coast, Fourth Genre, Boulevard.*

Many thanks to the Artist Trust of Washington state, for a grant that
enabled me to complete a portion of this book.

for B. and J.,
for whom the world must be wonderful:
to match them

Contents

I now am made to Speak, because I am almost
weary of Speaking, and to informe the world
that Silence hath taken hold of my spirit.

Testimony of a Ranter

What is a Cassill? A case full of vomit.
What is a Cassill? A case full of vomit.

Bajan schoolboys' chant

Body
Toxic

Chapter One

First Words

In nineteen question-mark question-mark my silent grandfather came to the United States.

He left the hot chatty island of Barbados and because he existed in silence no one knows when he came. He came for shade. To drink tea-colored liquor we poured out, that scoured the tin sink. To watch every Saturday, as he did until he died, American cartoons like *Rocky & Bullwinkle*. He came to father my silent mother and find an America that seemed less like a place than an anti-place, a not-Barbados, not-Europe, not Asia or Africa, not meals of boiled monkey and *coocoo* or potatoes rotted bitter and Argus-eyed in the ground. Not this, not that.

My grandfather succeeded because silence succeeds. It can't be argued against. It is the last word.

My grandfather, Louis Cassill, came from an Anglophone island to an English-speaking country, where people were like radios that couldn't be turned off. I think he would have preferred a place that babbled nonsense in his ears. He sat alone and kept his pale amphibian eyes averted. He slammed the door in the faces of solicitors and Jehovah's Witnesses and Latter-Day Saints. He avoided even hellos and goodbyes, first cousins of speech.

On the other side of my family, the Antonettas, my greatgrandparents came with no English and an Italian dialect only people from the same group of villages could understand. They floated in the bubbles of their own thought, leaving behind tenant farming, earthquakes and cholera. They came because people in that part of Italy had begun coming to the U.S. to work, sending money home, planning to return to Italy, as the U.S. began pocking its face with factories and blowing into its air the hard breath of day labor.

My grandfather on this side put the television on when he woke up in the morning and didn't turn it off till he went to sleep. He didn't change channels much and when I saw him the TV always followed a natural and inevitable evolutionary path, daytime soaps to news to sitcoms and talk shows. My grandfather, whose name was Rafael and who everyone called Ralph, floated against a backdrop of daylit people dramatically fighting and cheating and falling into each other's arms again, and then bland, real murder and exploding Vietnamese villages at twilight, and nervous taped bizarrely repetitive laughter at night. Rafael called Ralph moved in front of that like a character in an old movie pretending to drive in front of a flat unrolling landscape. He only read papers like the *Weekly World News* and the *Star* and never understood much about what was going on in the world.

My aunt Philomena told me once that when my greatgrandfather came here he'd heard of the streets paved with gold and had no idea of the metaphor involved; he took a boat, steerage on a steamer, and emerged from the underdecks, from the Ellis Island ferry, to stare horrified? disgruntled? unsurprised really? at the disappointing asphalt of New York. He went, an older man, to Brooklyn, where my West Indian grandfather would soon arrive. My Cassill grandfather came with a mother who fled debt and a bad reputation. He talked about this country, when he did, as open space.

"New Jersey was a cow pasture then," he'd say irritatedly. "There was nothing at Holly Park. Nothing."

He had little feeling for nature—I never knew him to go outside without a reason, like fixing the well—but he resented the arrival to any place of human beings other than himself. In spite of that he had children.

Neither man could pass up the chance to breed American children, American progeny.

(Memoranda): I am Susanne Louise Antonetta. Right about now I am about 4'11" and weigh between 85–90 lbs. I live in the United States, at 345 East Washington Street . . . I have brown hair, brown eyes, and wear a size 8 shoe. (3/11/68, age 11)

I started keeping a diary when I was eleven. Someone had given me the diary of Anne Frank, with its foreword by Eleanor Roosevelt, and the book infected me with audience. I had always written for myself, plays and poems and stories: a weakness bred into me by my soft life in America. Now I pictured girls propped up with my book in their lap. Presidents' wives, bored, crusading. This audience changed my voice. I move from entries like

And white lipstick is a *must*

to what must have seemed the closest I could come to literary English, the strained diction of my English grandmother, the woman who married my West Indian grandfather.

> I think I shall write memoirs about life in America, and my philosophy and opinions about it. Then I will wrap it in mud or clay, and someday I shall bury it for people far in the future to find.

My aunt Philomena, my father's sister, tells a story about running up to her grandmother's apartment, on the top floor of the brownstone where three generations of the family lived in Brooklyn, to borrow an onion. She asked for it in English.

"*SHE-pole, SHE-pole*," my greatgrandmother screamed furiously— "onion" in their dialect—and flapped her hands to indicate she didn't understand my aunt, didn't speak a word of English.

"Oh, you're a stupid old woman," my aunt said, in English, whereon my greatgrandmother yelled downstairs in Italian that Philomena had just called her a stupid old woman.

My Cassill grandfather would have done the same thing, if he could possibly have pretended that Barbados was a non-English-speaking island. As it was, he had a field around him that bounced off conversation.

> I've been thinking of writing a story about a girl a lot like me, one that didn't have a happy ending. I want to write reality, not myth. The ending will be sad, but it will contain philosophy. (2/13/68, age 11)

> I'm making up a list of the 10 most appealing words I know. Here are some candidates: photograph, phone, cents, choice, crystal, fish (believe it or not!), love, hope, list, sweet, charm, paw, rose, beauty, breasts, and soft. (7/12/68, age 11)

A photographed fish: crystal. A choice phone. A fish made of crystal listing with love. Beauty breasted. Hopeful.

O rose thou are sweet, charmed, soft.

O rose thou art pawed.

My earliest diary, from the year I turned eleven, has a cover of plastic faux leopard skin, very 1960s. I must have had a strong sense of my words as type, because I wrote for a while in the closest writing I could manage to a plain typeface like Univers—the uncoordinated eleven-year-old version—even slanting some words very far to the right, one letter at a time, to indicate I wanted them to be italic.

My leopard diary had a key. I remember it: tiny and delicate and lovely slipping the little tumblers of its lock. I kept it in a place so secret I can't remember, and when I found the diary a quarter century later (stuffed in some old boxes) I had to cut the strap binding it shut with scissors. I'd kept it locked against my parents—who would have read it and seen no irony in punishing me for invasions of their privacy—and my brother and my friends. Nervous of the Word. So I carefully turned the little lock every night and hid both key and diary though I clearly saw the diary as in some ways a public thing. I wrote from both angles: the fiction that I wrote for myself only

> For the past few days I've been thinking of giving you a name. Maybe Cindy. Or maybe Sue, since you really are a division of myself.
> (4/1/68, age 11)

and a chronic parenthetical note of nudging a reader along

> (In case you don't remember who "the kids in the back" are, see Jan. 7)

> (If that sounds like a rather dramatic opening, I tend to be rather dramatic sometimes—I enjoy it) (1/6/68, age 11)

It may have been the fantasy that I had a friend desperate to understand me. Or maybe I'd already learned to split myself off into the self and the critic—the one who acts and the one who watches, giving no quarter, too indifferent even to remember.

Both sides of my family had elaborate silences, mantras of unspeech: *You don't talk about it. You didn't talk about it then.* Disease. Death. Wrongdoing. The Four Horsemen of the Apocalypse could hoof us under without our protest. My uncle Vito, an ex-prizefighter with a sixth-grade education, bought an old garbage truck and arranged a route on Long Island where garbage collection was a Mob business.

"First comes the phone calls," my aunt remembers. "This voice: 'They'll find you face down in the East River.'

"Then they started to talk about the kids. Then comes this big black car, parked in front of the house, just sittin there, every morning."

My uncle sold the truck. I heard the story thirty years later, my aunt Phil (my beloved aunt) susurrating in my ear. *You don't talk about it, not those things.* My father's uncle Manfredo with the Shylocks and the both-somethings broken. My English grandmother with her dilly-dallying, her cabbage patches and her people no better than they ought to be who'd been born under the rose. Her husband who never told anyone how many siblings he'd had, where they were or how the dead had died. Barbados, which we never talked about except to say: it was British.

Both families, asked direct questions, often respond with ludicrous invention.

"We're kin to the Lord Carrington of the House of Lords," my grandmother would say.

"I'm in with the Rackets," my uncle Tony said. "What do you want? I can get you anything you want."

You see, sometimes I get so involved in my daydreams that I have to give myself a mental slap in the face. (3/6/68, age 11)

I've been daydreaming much too much lately. I make up these stories in which I'm always the heroine. And all day long, I add to them, mentally. This is very bad. It makes me lose contact with reality, I don't know what's going on. (5/21/69, age 12)

I know my father's family came through Ellis Island, maybe my mother's father too, though not my socially pretentious English grandmother, who came in as war bride to a then-naturalized citizen. I remember my relatives talking about Ellis Island, the torpid, raw, bored officials with shirt buttons open in the heat, who sat with half-eaten sandwiches and wanted you to answer their questions fast and easy, no matter what you said. I think it set a tone: the first they saw of the rules and opportunities of their new home. Along with sidewalks that could tarnish into asphalt from squares of pure value—the mutability, the alchemy, the lie of the place.

I asked my father why our people moved here and he said, "It's the land of opportunity."

Where it's clear that anything you don't want to say doesn't need to be said.

To my mother and father and their mothers and fathers the wonder of this country stayed a given. An anxious thing, to live within the object of desire. It became a national passion in the fifties: how we were coveted from the outside. We poured money into an air defense network, developing missiles and planes (secretly), arming many of them with nuclear weapons. Our intelligence reported a "missile gap"—Russian missiles, more missiles than we had, pointed at key targets in the United States. No more Washington Monument, Bloomingdale's, Times Square and the ball that plummets to make each new year. So we rushed to catch up. One promising nuclear missile designed by Boeing and Michigan Aerospace Research Center, called BOMARC, looked like a well-licked paintbrush with dorsal fins. Concrete bunkers flexed out of the ground in a remote part of New Jersey called New Egypt (in the middle of a sandy pine forest, where no one could see) in southern Ocean County, where the BOMARCs could stand launch-ready to intercept Soviet bombers. Secret bunkers for secret bombs: not many people knew we put nuclear warheads on anti-aircraft missiles. Though it turned out Russia didn't have many missiles after all. Still, the BOMARCs had been built, at a cost of $1 million apiece. They were hauled in caravan to New Egypt and frozen in their attitudes of contemplation.

World War I had just guns and cannons and tear gas and mustard gas. My Cassill grandfather fought in it under two different flags and met my grandmother when he got wounded, in the neck and in the fingers, and shipped to London, where she nursed him. She never loved him, she told me, or liked him (she hinted) but she loved the idea of America. Their marriage was a long affair of politesse, diplomacy and avoidance. They had four children. In 1932, when his children were young, my grandfather decided to buy some land in a part of the New Jersey Pine Barrens, on the coast, and build them a cabin.

He arrived as he tended to do on the heels of disaster. The Barrens had always been poor, a million acres of unproductive land both boggy and sandy: a place for people hiding out. It had a brief boom, though, in the start of the twentieth century. Something about belief in the healing powers of pinesmell and seabrine. In the twenties slappedup buildings held balls and the Astors came, in fox fur (those rich enough to wear eternity around their necks, uroboros, head eating tail) and their own beautiful rich skin. In 1926 a developer built a subdivision of small cottages on a peduncle of coast land, a subdivision designed to be summer homes for up-and-coming New Yorkers. He named it Holly Park. In 1929 the stock market crashed and those New Yorkers ceased to exist (as the developer knew them) and the property reverted to its pre-boom values of $20 or $30 a lot.

Nearby this subdivision, a symbol of enduring poverty brushed up against, transformed by and then dropped from the coattails of greatness, my Cassill grandfather chose our land. When he finished jury-rigging up our cottages (there were two) my grandmother took the children and rewarded him by spending summers there, leaving him in the north, to make it down on weekends when he could.

(Every morning first thing my grandmother crossed the gravel road. As she crossed the road her spirit rose and kited out of her life. She threw off her cotton shift and the hydraulic system that was 1930s women's underwear, and skinnydipped for a long time in Barnegat Bay. Still her children weren't allowed to use the words "pregnant" or "God.")

Separation and separation and separation.

Ocean County eats into the hourglass of New Jersey in a triangular bite, smooth on the land sides and rough on the third that fronts the water. Down the Atlantic side runs a long peninsula, akimbo like an arm but too skinny: a humerus and radial of peninsula. This peninsula cuts off the Atlantic and forms our bay, Barnegat. Because of its position Island Beach holds the county's valuable property—good surf, sand beaches, boardwalks—though it makes up a tiny percentage of the land. Our bay tends to stagnate and grow what look like floating molds and mildews. Rather than sand beaches we have marshes and weeds spreading up to the water. Swimming's lackluster as is fishing; crabbing's good. We always had the things that needed cover and barrier to grow: crabs, cranberries, blackberries, the secret pleasures. Most people in New Jersey considered the Barrens ugly, with its monotonous landscape of sparsely needled pitch and scrub pines, cattails and bogs.

When my grandfather came to this area, Holly Park in Berkeley Township in south Ocean County, only a few thousand people lived there. Island Beach hadn't been developed much. There were very few jobs and people often lived in ways inconceivable in the rest of the state, catching and picking their food, making charcoal and gathering cranberries, slapping together their shelter. As my grandfather did.

The bungalows my grandfather built faced a small inlet of Barnegat Bay and backed onto a large lagoon that kept the plain rooms awhine with mosquitoes.

My family and my aunts and uncles and cousins spent most of our summers there. We still go, now and then. I feel that place in my ear, in a spot where it cannot be slapped.

By the time I existed and had memory, someone had taken the unpromising curve of land along our side of the inlet and built a wooden bulkhead along it, with a few piers for crabbing. A piece of land the size of a housing lot in a subdivision tolerated the dumping of much clayey sand and served as a beach. It had steps leading into the water. Ostensibly this was a private beach—nearby families gave a few dollars a year and got badges my mother and my aunts fussed about but nobody remembered to wear. An old wooden building had been thrown up by the gate, where someone had the job of beach-keeper, always somebody old and sagging and bristly in a bathing suit: tensed to run my cousins and my brother and me off. We were bad children, and flooded the beach by damming the baby pool drain with carefully packed layers of clay and rocks.

We loved things that soaked and flooded, or seared and burned and wizened. Firecrackers. Matchbombs. And the bleached remarkably infertile soil of the Barrens, like sand but close enough to clay to clump in your hands; we could (and did) sit at the beach and construct elaborate cities. Next to our house was a field of cattails, with maybe a redwinged blackbird or two bobbing on a tassel. Smallish and spindly needled pines, white cedars here and there, ash; a sparse tree line and brackish water, so weedy it looked like a cauldron of wigs.

> I've been down the shore a week now. I just love it down here. Especially the lagoon in the back. It is beautiful. The grass is long there, and its bent to the side, so that from far away it looks like velvet.

I loved to be there, loved the greens and blues and the sense of open space, even as it all filled me with a desire to tear apart.

> There is also snake-grass, which is multi-colored green & gold. When the wind blows, it looks like gold is rippling through it. I love the snake-grass, but it makes me very sad. I remember the first time I ever went there. I was young & wearing shorts. Now the snake-grass has a very sharp tip, which will cut you if you don't wear pants. I went through a patch of snake-grass, and came out with legs covered with innumerable tiny cuts. It was almost like it was saying, "go home—you don't belong here."

My grandfather built the larger house on concrete blocks like stilts, with a three feet high space under the house, damp and dark and stinking: mud, brine, septic system. We kids played there. It always seemed to be housing the feral: a wild cat we called Mama Cat because she had kittens there every year, a muskrat I fed that dragged back one day with a bullet in its gut.

> I don't like the word "lagoon." It sounds like something ugly.
> (6/27/70, age 13)

Lots of local people hunted muskrat for pelts and meat.

———

We call the houses the Big Bungalow and the Little Bungalow, or the Little Cottage and Big Cottage. They have no heat and had no hot water until I was out of childhood, when we put hot water and a shower into the Little Bungalow. Before then we took cold showers at the beach, along the side of the beachhouse, or sponged off from the sink. We boiled teakettles of water for dishwashing. The Little Bungalow, basically two tiny bedrooms and a toilet, has a flat roof that always had a wooden ladder leaning against it and made a favorite play area, especially at night, when you could see stars and stay slightly above the densest layer of mosquitoes.

The Big Bungalow has a galley kitchen, a living room/dining room space: big table covered with oilcloth, a woodframe sofa with mildewy whiskeycolored cushions. Two bedrooms lie in the back, one with two sets of bunkbeds and the blue table that is possessed. In the forties or fifties my grandfather added a porch in front to provide extra sleeping space.

The houses stand one behind the other, painted the green of pea soup or old khaki.

Here are sounds: the thrush of wind in the cattails, the shredding American flag snapping on the beach, sounding like a solemn flagellation. There might be swings instead of empty chains on the decrepit swing set and if so, they skreek by themselves.

Odors: two notes of bay and lagoon. Around the inlet in the half-circle the bulkhead doesn't reach cattails grow to the ruff of washedup seaweed at the edge of the water, several feet of it knit with dead and dying fish and shellfish, moss bunkers, blueclaws, horseshoe crabs in the old days, maybe flipped over and straining their ladders of little claws. The lagoon's black stagnant mosquito trenches and greasy gunmetal soil. Marshgas, brine, dead things, too much breeding.

———

In 1960 (June), a tank in a BOMARC bunker caught fire, in New Egypt, fifteen miles or so from our houses. The fire fed on the TNT in the missile detonators and burned out of control and the nuclear warhead dropped into the molten mass of the rest, which flamed for nearly an hour. Radioactive particles spread over the ground and the groundwater. Firefighters' hoses rained pools of plutonium-laced water. About a pound of plutonium was left there, too radioactive to move. In 1972 the government, answering cries for protection, installed a chainlink fence to protect civilians.

Psycho had been released that summer—my parents and aunts and uncles went to see it. The movie posters featured Janet Leigh and Alfred Hitchcock and, especially, Alfred Hitchcock's finger, pointing upward to the title, or held in a silencing gesture to his lips. Nobody was supposed to talk about *Psycho*. My parents came home unable to sleep. Hitchcock had decided to make the cheapest movie he could make, black-and-white, no special props, and my elders came home terrified, possessed by visions of Janet Leigh pretending to die in a puddle of chocolate syrup.

I ask my parents if they remember the BOMARC fire and they don't. I ask them if they remember *Psycho* and they do.

"That bastard movie," says my dad, who loves to swear.

I almost never wrote diary entries at the shore—I have just three or four, so my summer days ruffle on, blank, as if they never happened. I brought a diary with me everywhere else but sleeping in my place— the bottom lefthand bunk in the back bedroom of the Big House—I probably had nowhere to hide it. My cousins would have taken it, or my brother, or my parents and uncles and aunts.

By my twelfth year my diary changes a lot, losing the fantasy of audience. No print, just furious rolling littlegirl script, and no internal references. No Cindy, just "Dear Diary," though I included the salutation and signed my name no matter how little I had to say.

> Dear Diary,
> Oh God!
> Susanne (5/2/69, age 12)

No matter how moody—I feel aful. Today has totally confirmed yesterday's lamentations. Right now I feel as if I'm leading such a happy life!—my entries still maintain that formality, always on the page under the right date, abruptly cut off if I ran out of room. I felt a responsibility. A sense of purpose. I apologized on and on for my silences, as if someone would be hurt by the blankness of August 6, 1969. I wrote detailed descriptions of practically nothing, grass or cattails or

> a sand "city" & a reservoir system for it. It was pretty clever. First, there was a main stream of water coming down from the baby pool, which ended in a deep water hole. Against this water hole was a large dam. From this main stream of water branched three deep water holes, to drain water from the stream & keep too much pressure off the dam. Behind the dam was a deep, unfilled lake, so that if the dam broke, the water would go into it. All of the walls were high, sturdy; of mud, but the dam was the strongest of all. It had a base of driftwood, plastered with mud, and strengthened with stones & seaweed. Beyond that lay the city, with a drive-in, a department store, school, & lots of pretty little houses, all of sand. Sincerely, Susanne

—someone chokeholding her existence, finding it improbable, vital in its parts and slipping.

When I asked my mother how long the DDT trucks had driven past our cottages she said since she was a girl, which shows the obsessiveness of memory mingled with repetition; after a certain number of times seeing a thing the image reproduces in your head, wildly, like cells in a cancer. My mother was twelve in 1932 when her father built the cottages. DDT arrived commercially in 1942, making my mother at least twenty-two. I don't blame her usually dry and precise memory. I feel like those trucks powdered me in the womb.

They came once a week or so, supplemented by planes: a spume, a round gray meteorological event of pesticide. The trucks stopped only when the United States banned DDT in the seventies. A local man, an environmentalist named Willie DeCamp, remembers a lamewinged robin touched down on his front steps in Mantoloking when the truck went by, the bird twittering, dead after.

In 1952, four years before the year at the end of which I squeezed into the world, the Ciba-Geigy Chemical Corporation bought 1,400 acres along Toms River, a nearby river feeding into Barnegat Bay. Ciba-Geigy chose this land, marshy, scrubbily woodsy with longtailed grass, for an operations site, as distinct from its corporate headquarters in New York. Cheap, eager labor, lots of useless land for landfill. The low buildings churned out commercial dyes and epoxy resins and plastics, and chemical waste byproducts. These last were disposed of in various ways: in 14,000 drums buried and stored in nonhazardous waste landfills lined with plastic wrap; in a pipeline that a former employee said led from one building straight into the woods, dumping cyanide in the ground; in liquid waste pumped in an underground pipeline built beneath Barnegat Bay into the Atlantic Ocean, a mile from a public beach.

In 1984, armed with search warrants, the New Jersey Division of Criminal Justice raided the Ciba-Geigy plant and spent two days collecting samples and searching.

A long investigation concluded that Ciba-Geigy left a plume of contamination in the aquifer, the natural underground water system that provided drinking water: a poison plume a mile square and dozens of feet deep, containing ninety-five different chemicals. A migratory plume. A strange new life like a huge amoeba. The Environmental Protection Agency is trying to pump it out but estimates it will be there another thirty to fifty years.

Ciba-Geigy also used its pipeline to transport military waste, including nuclear waste, for a base in nearby Lakehurst. The pipeline ruptured in April 1984 at the intersection of residential Bay and Vaughn Avenues in Toms River, spewing out a puddle of toxins.

Two and a half decades later that spot on the map is the center of a cluster of childhood cancers of the brain and nervous system. Dozens of children are dying, some of rare cancers that may cause them to stay four feet tall into their teens, or distend their skulls, eggplantlike, with tumors. The Centers for Disease Control are there. The Agency for Toxic Substances and the Environmental Protection Agency are there. A half-dozen federal agencies are studying the cluster, with money specially allocated by Congress.

"Some mistakes were made in the past," confessed C-G spokesman Glenn Ruskin.

The EPA list of Ciba-Geigy toxins goes on for four single-spaced near-marginless pages, alphabetical, from acetone to zinc, a list including heavy metals and pesticides.

We lived something like four miles from Ciba-Geigy, though I don't recall knowing it was there. We knew Toms River, of course, the next town and nearest big one, a place to row and to swim.

A mile or so north of us, a company called Denzer & Schafer X-Ray operated a site that made money by reclaiming the silver found in old negatives, painstakingly dissolving strips of images. Chemical stripping solutions leached the metal out. The company used its septic system, illegally, to dispose of the stripping solutions. Denzer & Schafer did this for seven years, filling our aquifer with lead. Also arsenic, chromium and mercury; D&S left a total of forty-four EPA-chronicled chemicals.

The D&S plant was close to Potter's Creek, where we crabbed and fished, on the Bayville Road, where we walked to pick berries and sassafras roots, and just to walk.

> We walked for 2 miles thru desolate land, with no houses around, just cat-tails and bushes. We walked til we came to an old dirt road where Mark told us that old men came with their whores. 2 girls were raped & murdered a while back. Helen & I were getting pretty scared.

In the same way that I collected words I collected experiences, or bits of experiences, as much as I could get.

> We both took a stone from it.
> Mine is a cream-colored, small stone, pinched at the center, & not very pretty.

Those roads were unbelievably dark at night: a collection of rattling whooing noises in a black bowl. I can see this stone glowing a little there, disappointing when I got home.

> But we got in shits of trouble for being out so late.　(7/19/70, age 13)

Here's another story, of a man who grew wealthy. His name is Nicholas Agricola, and because of his name I assume someone in his family came from elsewhere to find the brilliant sidewalks of the United States. Maybe not. Anyway, Agricola started his own hauling business. In the 1960s (the go-go sixties, economists call them) Agricola got a contract from Union Carbide to dispose of drums of hazardous waste for $3.50 a drum. The waste came from plants elsewhere in the state, and it consisted of chemical byproducts from the making of plastic for, among other things, Bic pens. Agricola hauled away some 7,000 drums of waste, dutifully, coming back empty, earning a small fortune in sixties money.

Then on an old farm called Reich Farm (a few miles from us, off the road) the absentee owner decided to look over his property and found his fallow land blooming: with some 5,000 drums stamped with the name Union Carbide. He had leased his land, it turned out, to Nicholas Agricola. Drums leaked. Trenches, dug like our mosquito trenches, oozed with loose sludge. This was in 1971. The Reich Farm site too feeds into our aquifer and has made its own plume, with an EPA list of toxins that goes on for pages, from acetone to trichloroethylene. Two municipal wells draw water from this plume.

Much later, several thousand more Union Carbide drums were found in the Dover Township Landfill to the south, same stuff from the same period, also leaching into the groundwater.

The northern chemical companies had run out of room, room where no one would notice corroding drums and oozing sludge pits. They didn't seem to think anyone would mind.

"Oh yeah," my mother says philosophically. "Everyone dumped their stuff back there, on the old chicken farms."

"They did? How do you know?"

She answers guardedly, "We used to take walks." She won't tell me any more.

Nicholas Agricola admitted to dumping at both sites and was fined, according to the head of a Toms River organization for parents of children with cancer, $100. He kept his money and his story has a simple ending.

———

Being Americans, we don't just dump toxins into our soils but catalogue them, create hierarchies. We have for that the Environmental Protection Agency, which creates lists: lists of sites to watch and investigate, to ignore, to give up on, lists of the worst sites in the United States, the ones that pose an immediate danger. The last would be the National Priorities List, and to deal with these and lesser but also bad sites Congress created a special project called the Superfund.

In 1982 wells in Berkeley Township and Beachwood Borough were placed on the National Priorities List. Testing had found lead in many of them, and the EPA report also lists high quantities of chloride, copper, manganese, nitrate and sulfate. Supposedly all wells were tested and many houses required to tap into the municipal water lines, though our well was never tested. Our bungalows never seemed to exist in any consciousness outside the family's; we also had no street address (rumors ran that our street was named Main Street, but there'd never been a street sign) and did not get mail. It made me wonder if my grandfather had built them illegally, or if he'd put some Bajan spell on us, and made us invisible.

In the fifty United States, Puerto Rico, Guam, the U.S. Virgin Islands and other protectorates like the Mariana Islands lie about 1,100 National Priorities List sites, the worst of the Superfund. One hundred and eleven of these live and leach in New Jersey, making the state, as the *Asbury Park Press* once boasted in a very East Coast way (what won't we brag about?), maybe the most toxic known spot in the world. Though anyone who's driven along the New Jersey Turnpike would find this unlikely, most NPLs lie in the south, in poor rural areas like southern Ocean County, where dumping has been profitable and easy. They also happen to be places where drinking water comes from an underground, easily reached aquifer rather than a reservoir.

Three adjoining counties—Ocean, Monmouth and Burlington—
had by the nineties the most National Priorities List sites, twelve,
twelve and thirteen, respectively. Lots of these sites have postcardy
country names: Bog Creek Farm, Reich Farm, Burnt Fly Bog. Burlington County's one site up on Ocean but is much larger, making Ocean
and Monmouth Counties rivals for the prize of most documented
contaminants. Not to mention the sites like the Dover Township
Landfill that should be on the National Priorities List but aren't because their investigations drag on, year and year after year.

The numbers work out elegantly: we have more than 10% of New
Jersey's 10% of the swills scattered over tens and tens of thousands of
American places.

I spent a lot of my eleventh and twelfth years pining for my menstruation to begin. I can't remember why.

(Oh, if only I can have my menstruation. Jr. High will be perfect)

My women friends tell me they remember feeling that way, but
I don't. I remember the time after, which I also recorded: my life
ordered by the demands of the Kotex, the only permissible thing for
half-Catholic girls in New Jersey to use. The flowery little cases for
your purse. The garter belt that held napkins in place, a garish sexual
sign that cradled its small white chastity belt.

I went straight to girl's room and Alice saved my seat. I carried the nap-
kin in in a paper bag, so it looked like my lunch. But I bought my lunch.
We have disposers in my school but they don't work. (2/7/69, age 12)

I write on and on about each menstruating schoolday, like there's
nothing more public than blood: I could barely contain it.

Ocean County has a nuclear power plant that's not a simple story. Built in 1969, the Oyster Creek reactor is the oldest nuclear power plant still operating and the only Mark I boiling water reactor design left in service. It has released the most or the second most (depending on who you talk to) nuclear fission materials of any plant in the country into the atmosphere—venting, for instance, 77 curies of iodine-131 and particulates during the seventies and eighties, when the industry average was one or two.

In 1976 three nuclear engineers who worked for General Electric, the plant's designer and operator, quit the company in protest over safety problems. They wrote a seventy-page report detailing their concerns and asked to speak to Congress's Joint Committee on Atomic Energy. The group included the man responsible for performance evaluation of GE's Mark I boiling water reactors, Dale Bridenbaugh.

"I was not assessing the safety of plants—I was doing whatever I could to make sure they kept operating," he testified at the congressional hearing.

The men—Richard Hubbard, Gregory Minor and Bridenbaugh—also testified about a design flaw that causes a shock wave to spread through the reactors' coolant water during loss of coolant accidents—leading the torus, which holds up the reactor core, to jump and drop back down. The men recommended that Mark I's be reevaluated and stressed the "severe hazard" of nuclear plants to the public.

Along with the General Electric engineers a project manager for the Nuclear Regulatory Commission, Robert Pollard, resigned and testified with them. He talked about the way, at the agency regulating nuclear power, keeping reactors open and on schedule "frequently prevailed over reactor safety."

Pollard went on to say of nuclear power, "I believe the American people are being misled."

Boiling water reactors use water to cool down the reactor core, and some of that water becomes radioactive steam. In the Mark I design the steam's held in a holdup tank for a short while to allow the worst radionuclides to decay, then vented into the atmosphere.

The Oyster Creek reactor—under the ownership of General Public Utilities, which also owned Three Mile Island—logged one of the largest releases of radioactive gas on record in 1979, when pipes broke and coolant water levels dropped. By the mid-1980s our county ranked fourth in the nation for radioactive emissions in the air.

Dale Bridenbaugh later talked to journalists about the way plants operated. Not neat as they'd been sold to the public, but alive and oozing. He recalled plants shipping radioactive liquids in crates lined with Kotex. ("We bought Kotex by the truck-load, almost by the rail-road-car-full. What keeps a nuclear plant running is lots of Kotex, lots of masking tape, and lots of plastic bags.")

Oyster Creek's still there, five miles upwind of our cottages, on my grandmother's favorite gooseberry patch. We continued to pick there. The plant sucks cooling water in from Forked River, which it's built along, and ejects it—warmed and now holding small amounts of radioactivity—back out into Oyster Creek. The filters at the intake and output pipes act like strainers on a vacuum cleaner, sucking up billions of fish eggs and larva, whole fish, crabs, whatever, and reducing them to a chum of dead sealife. Fish, especially a local fish called moss bunker, swarm around the plant, happy if they don't get vacuumed, stagnant in the water with their mouths open feeding on the pablum the plant spits out. Bunkers love the warm water temperatures. They should be a migratory fish but stay all year. They think we're Florida. In each scram or shutdown the water temperature drops suddenly and thousands of dead bunkers float, squat and silver, in the river and the bay.

A local highway bridge crosses the river and on any given day it's packed with fishermen, with oldstyle tight jeans and t-shirts over shelved bellies and coolers of beer (Schlitz in south Jersey, or Rolling Rock), whose poles reach into the power plant waters, reeling in the warm, stupid fish.

Scientists from a group called The Radiation and Public Health Project are collecting old baby teeth now, in Ocean County: dug out of the keeping of sentimental moms, cleaned and dropped into little envelopes. They're shoving the teeth under scintillating counters to measure levels of radioisotopes like strontium-90. They're doing this to measure the effects of Oyster Creek, a reactor they consider one of the world's worst.

Already, says Jay Gould, a nuclear scientist who's running the project, "we have results you can't explain with fallout from atmospheric testing."

Each tooth takes seven hours to gauge completely. The counters twitch and twitch, like stranded crabs wrapped in kelp on the shoreline.

The Tooth Fairy Project drew funding from the Rockefeller Foundation and got the support of Alec Baldwin, an actor/environmentalist, a handsome man from a handsome family, of men with dazzling teeth. When families got their letters asking them to dig through jewelry boxes and part with baby teeth the letters came under the signature of Alec Baldwin, a man whose smile doctors hoped would get mothers to part with the molars and canines and bicuspids they'd carefully saved, in jeweler's velvet or plastic wrap or cotton wool.

———

While I grew up the quartersized frogs I spent my early childhood catching, housing in shoeboxes and letting go disappeared, along with the horseshoe crabs, the snapping turtles, clams, most of the valuable fish like fluke. They left while my puberty came, as if my womb itself released them. The monarch butterflies disappeared, with their orange and black stripes, like the covers of a book. Everything left, just about, but the mosquitoes, which thrived. Chemicals like DDT and chlordane are endocrine disruptors, which cause things like defeminization of females and demasculinization of males, hermaphrodism, blurring of sex characteristics; loss of species through loss of reproduction.

The Catholic Church has a theme of the grief of souls divided from bodies by abortion or contraception: the soul as two parts separated by a wall, a latex wall or a flesh one, the ovum tricked into staying in the ovary. Nobody has taken up the theme of the souls not getting that far, housed in shapeless eggs or weak sperm, swimmy and lost, diverted by chemicals.

Environmentalists talk about "sacrifice communities"—what the Citizens Awareness Network calls areas "generally poor and rural" chosen to house our toxic waste and nuclear power. Our area had pineys and immigrants, and to the latter the place just looked like America: uncrowded, unclaimed, able to glow in the right light. Until recently you could buy a decent piece of land in Berkeley Township for a few thousand dollars. The median household income in 1990 was $23,000. We were chosen, in a way that sounds almost like a religious calling.

My brother and my cousin Mark and I formed a terrorist group: the Environmental Liberation Army, or the ELA. We were sincere terrorists and very much in the sixties mode of talking about our terrorism and creating manifestos, though we were something like ten, twelve and fourteen at the time. When *For Sale* signs went up in the pinewoods we spraypainted them with "We Will Stop You! ELA" or "ELA Will Avenge." Sometimes we wrote out Environmental Liberation Army, aping the Symbionese Liberation Army and the Students for a Democratic Society. We thought if we could convince people there were hundreds of us, armed and dangerous, they might stop.

We noticed the shipworms breeding in the warmed water, the docks that collapsed, the missing butterflies and dying fish. Our parents went on, forbidding us to swim after lunch, freshly poured tonic water popping in their hands. It felt to us like our parents did not notice, rapt in the significations of class and leisure, following Hitchcock's finger.

"My wife's family's got a place at the shore," my father liked to say.

When he could find the beds he dragged his side of the family down. We drove my grandfather Ralph to the Atlantic because he insisted—he hated Barnegat Bay—and then he'd stand in the thrashing surf and scream at it, stop! stop! with his hand up.

In the seventies, eighties and nineties the Toms River/Beachwood area has been wracked by childhood cancers—particularly of the brain and nervous system—leukemias, breast cancers, many times higher than normal. My family was not. We've been wracked by infertility, tumors, organs malformed at birth and manic-depression.

As a diarist I learned patience and frustration. Maybe I started the job with frustration, because my diary tends to have an underlying hint of frenetic whine. I choked facts but they choked me back; they stuck, like Legos—clingy but hard to build into anything real. I can know what hung in the water, nested in the soft tissues of the fish. I can't look into the novel of my body and go to the end, where it tells what happened. I have or have had one spectacular multiple pregnancy, a miscarriage, a radiation-induced tumor, a double uterus, asthma, endometriosis, growths on the liver, other medical conditions like allergies.

Here are tales of cause and effect:

After low-level radioactive releases in Hanford, Washington, exposed women developed double the rate of thyroid disease and spontaneous abortion (miscarriage).

In a medical study of workers exposed to low-level radiation the majority of the workers developed thyroid tumors.

After exposing female laboratory monkeys to dioxins and PCBs, those monkeys more often than not develop endometriosis.

Liver tumors like mine can be induced by too many industrial chemicals to list.

Low-level exposure to many pesticides causes kindling in the brains of laboratory mice—electrical misfiring, spikes and bursts of activity, like the firing you'd see in the brain of a manic-depressive.

Women in Taiwan, exposed to PCBs in their cooking oil, saw a sharp rise in birth defects.

Female mammals exposed to endocrine disruptors give birth to offspring with deformed sex organs.

Gerry Nicholls of the state Department of Environmental Protection admitted at a press conference that Ocean County well water contains manmade radiological particles, which once consumed begin degrading your body's cells, greedy for fresh electrons.

I have blood drawn all the time to monitor various things. I like to daydream while the vials rush and color about what's in there. Saltwater, red cells, ancestors braided and escaping. A bony geography.

Recently I learned from a researcher at the state Department of Environmental Protection that Berkeley Township along with another township in Ocean County is being investigated for a cluster of autistic children. "Where we should be seeing one or two we're seeing forty," he said. I keep speaking to researchers, at the EPA, the DEP, the Health Department. All say it's too early to tell anything but admit that pesticides can screw up a neurotransmitter called GABA, which regulates kindling and is implicated in autism. GABA is also implicated in manic-depression (GABA problems can be mapped in manic-depressive genes). In neurological terms the diseases function in similar ways.

No one's ever looked for patterns of manic-depression there, they tell me. It's too hard. Mark and I have the disorder. Maybe my grandfather, whose mind remains one of the most foreign places I've known.

> I'm going to avoid Mark like the plague in the future. He's a bad influence. Something's wrong with him. I won't go into it now, I don't want to talk about it. I'll just avoid him, that's all. (7/19/68, age 11)

When I first found my journals, ten years or so ago, the girl I found shocked me: her foreignness and her familiarity. I had believed that as a girl I felt normal.

> Today, I don't want to say much. I'm all confused & I don't know—I just don't know. I keep terrifying myself by imagining that I got my ESP from the Devil & he's going to claim my soul for it when I die. And something way down inside me keeps kicking up & being rebellious & demanding something & I don't know what it wants. That program went good & I didn't mess up or anything but that little Something inside me isn't satisfied. (6/17/68, age 11)

> Sometimes I think that maybe Earth is an experiment created by scientists on some other world. Or Mom, Dad, Chris and everyone else is in some hideous conspiracy against me. (6/22/69, age 12)

So many things have been disappearing lately. I'm so afraid I'm mentally ill. There are times when I just seem to blank out. God, I'm so scared. (6/17/70, age 13)

Written in a quick desperate scrawl, no neatness, no handy references to other times I blanked out. My grammar reverting to something closer to the way I talked.

I would love to be able to cast our minds into that landscape, if not the poisons then the spirit that lives there. I want reason. It took a lot out of us to learn to live without being able to think right, at least not all the time, though one of us (why lie now? it was me) found narcotics could still the tooth. For a while.

In the second month I kept a diary, I wrote

You know, what I write down is so uninteresting. I suppose I was thinking of a book, "The Diary of Anne Frank." The book is about a Jewish girl in World War II (or was it I?). Actually, it's a copy of her diary. It's not made up, either, it's true. Sometimes I hope that someone will find my diary when I'm dead, and publish it.

Of course the girl who wrote this did die, done in by a multitude of killers: time, puberty, modern pharmaceuticals.

Getting back to the uninteresting point of view. I've never been in a tornado or hurricane. I've never hidden myself from Nazis or Russians or Red Chinese, or anything like that.

Here I'm in that mode of preciously neat, Univers printing. A lot of diarists say they don't trust themselves. I tell my stories and I do trust myself but I know my mind has been declared legally untrustworthy, like a well on Reich Farm with a sign hung around it.

If there were blood tests for place all I can see is a brackish test tube with a kelp strand, moss bunkers like fat minnows on their sides, and frogs with ova and testes, both useless.

I'm just a normal, every-day, commonplace New Jersey-ian.
(2/27/68, age 11).

This, I feel certain, is a truth.
Perhaps I'll tell.

Postscript: 1974

It's my brother's Spider summer. Not dog days but spider days. It's 1974 and things have been crashing. Nixon's resigned or is going to and a few years ago Apollo 13 crash-landed when an oxygen tank blew (astronauts in there like Spam in a can, Chuck Yeager said). Karen Silkwood's about to crash. My brother has a blue Fiat (Fix It Again Tony) Spider. It has no backseat but I ride in the back anyway, rolled up in the ten inches or so under the rear window. Spiders aren't much more than humansized tins so this is risky but it doesn't matter. I am a lost person. Let me be a bottle rocket.

I ride to the shore with my brother and his college roommate Charly, barreling down the Garden State Parkway with my face smeared into the window like a child's, staring at the stars out of necessity and not sentiment. They're scattered but stuck, like something fine's holding them. I'm the no-backseat backseat person because my body's gaunt from years of narcotics.

Once I had a brilliant hallucination, realer than real life. Like dreamreal and real-real glued together. In it I rotated in a clear bubble through empty space, waving at people who rotated by in their clear bubbles waving at me. I felt like Buzz Aldrin, my favorite astronaut because he came from New Jersey and his mother's name was Marion Moon.

My brother bought his Spider to drive to Trenton, where he has a summer job with the state Department of Environmental Protection. He was hired to replace somebody whose job was running tests on samples of possibly contaminated water. The first day somebody bored showed him around, his lab, his desk, his samples. It turned out the man he replaced quit working four or five years ago though he kept coming in and getting paid. The lab hung with spiderwebs, dust like moondust (moondust smells "just like gunpowder," Buzz Aldrin said). Chris wondered what the guy'd been doing with himself and opened cabinets and desk drawers to discover years of pornography: *Hustlers*, *Playboys*, *Penthouses*, sliding heaps of the stuff. Books with stories about women who had perfect melons and steaming love ovens. He spent a few days cleaning out the porn and spiders and started on the four or five years' worth of water samples. (Some he thinks were contaminated—lead, mercury—most were not. Most, according to a toxicologist I know, would have degraded after five years and become untestable anyway.)

Chris and I find his job hilarious and create a history for the lost guy, who spent the past five years in a state of bored sexual arousal. We don't make up a history for the water sample people, who still drink their water, arcing it over ground coffee or mixing it with tubes of frozen juice. They do it however I make them do it but the fact is, they drink. At the shore Denzer & Schafer starts dumping into our ground and groundwater leftover arsenic, chromium, lead, mercury, chloroform, and it begins its underearth pilgrimage to wherever.

What was it Buzz Aldrin said? Earth looks beautiful from here, I think. Neil Armstrong said, Like a big blue eyeball staring right at me.

Chapter Two

Little
Squalicum

My grandfather told us about the drowned men and he laughed.

They were not his drowned, his greatuncle the smuggler had drowned them, but still he felt proprietary toward them, as though he might have drowned them, and so he laughed. We laughed too, we children, because he seemed to be passing them on. I think of these sinking minstrels as I walk along the licked freezing shore of the Puget Sound. In Barbados people will tell you the casuarina trees moan with the voices of the drowned, or even with the voices of women mourning their drowned. And the trees do moan, and I have no reason to doubt their explanation. Here, though, we have plenty of drowned, and only the silence of the madronas and Sitka spruce. There's the wind but that speaks in the voice of the murderer and not the victim. How then do we quiet our dead?

It's impossible for me to forget my grandfather; it's almost as hard to remember him. A spare man, dry and rimpled as a knee. He told very few stories. Most of the time his silence seemed unshakable, a vow, or one side of an explosive communication with things we couldn't see. I remember him—full nose and mouth in a palely ascetic face—but he hangs in memory with the solemn stupidity of portraiture. I can recall a nasal voice and laughter and the weird charm of the drowned men. But I can't make his lips move.

It's hard to know what to say about someone who wasn't larger than life, or smaller than life, but who simply seemed the antithesis of life.

Let me put it another way. From here I can see the Canadian Rockies. In the very blue air that hazes toward the edge the mountains themselves are blue, the same tentative horizon shade, with snowy peaks the even paler blue of the passing cirrus. The mountains here are impressive, as brochures tell you, sinewy as a muscled arm, harsh with glacial concavities. But they blur into the atmosphere. Sometimes the snowcaps seem to float above nothing but the vaguest hint of a shape. On these days when mountains melt into sky they draw even more clouds around them.

So my grandfather too could fade: had to wrap himself in the passing insubstantial.

We spent Christmas at my grandparents' house, my Cassill grandparents, me and my brother and six cousins. As soon as we kids saw each other some kind of chemical change occurred and we started running and screaming. It drove my grandmother crazy.

It interests me that even in a happy world, which I think ours is basically (or at least a world saturated with the possibility of happiness), children scream, always.

My grandfather Louis Cassill sat in a deep chair, a bulky armchair that made him look even smaller than he was. It felt odd to see him across the room, wrinkled and puppetlike, as if, watching us children steadily, he'd willed himself into our scale. He drank Manhattans from a jug he kept by his chair. I remember the shot glass moving up over and over again in his white hairy hand and its cargo of vermouth and whiskey draining into the otherwise stagnant space of the chair. Their molecules, forced to die into his, lived on in the afterworld of his odor. I recall that too, the bitter, startling, adult smell of liquor.

Most often my grandpa stayed silent. When he did talk he tended to tell, in the simple but heavily ironic voice he used for children, family stories like the one about the smuggler. He relished his Bajan family, with their easy dismissal of borders like earth and water, life and death. He wanted us to feel the same way, cueing us to laugh and we did, but uneasily. We thought of ourselves as Cassills, had been trained to think of ourselves as Cassills—the latest incarnation of these West Indians with their briny lives and homicidal ambitions. We knew it was really us he was talking about.

We kids ate in my grandparents' basement, things like Yorkshire pudding, bloody beef, what I thought of as pretend food because I wouldn't really eat it. The basement room smelled of must, with my grandmother's old looms set up at the ends, each holding the start of a knotted rug. The room felt like the inside of a body, deep within, and old. It was reddish in some way and smelled moldy but sicklysweet.

In the parlor we got gifts: big things—a camera, a ten-dollar bill—

for the two boys, Mark and my brother, Chris; a few dollars or a Barbie outfit for each of the six girls. We didn't expect more. It wasn't the presents we liked, but opening them—a glut of red-and-green paper that stubbornly repeated the ideas of candy canes, Santa Clauses, holly.

My grandpa sat without moving, as if he too was a narrative that couldn't be unstuck from a single image. He watched us from across the room, his eight weeds, his seeds in the world, and seemed to sink back, feeling maybe the vivid passings sap his form.

My brother always asked him how he was. "One foot in the grave," my grandfather said.

"Oh come on grandpa," my brother told him.

"One foot in the grave," my grandpa repeated, and finally smiled.

"A toast Louie," my grandmother said at the table and my grandfather would respond with, "To the bloody politicians, may they rot."

When I was a child very little in my purview bothered me as much as my grandfather's lower lip did. It dominated his face and jarred his saddish features: full and shiny, a lip that had migrated from another face and hung there, protruding, out of shape and out of spirits. My grandpa, pale eyed and small, had, like many West Indians, features that seemed sure in their ethnicity until you looked at them twice: Britty eyes, slightly kinked nose, the lip that didn't match its mate . . . he looked old, tufty and foldy, crease on crease. I don't remember him ever not looking old.

When my grandpa felt the urge to address someone he usually confined himself to the two boys.

"Don't trust the politicians," he said. "The hell with McNamara. Stay out of Veet-nam."

My grandfather liked to bring out his bloody jacket from World War I, unwashed, sweet and rotten with its uncouth map of the human veins, and tell the boys about getting shot. I think he looked on telling his grandsons about dying as a duty, as if dying were sex, something they would have to do and have done to them, and the jacket became like one of those sex books for kids, a handy anatomical reference. He encouraged them to handle it, know it, as you might help a boy understand the female body.

More than he hated anyone my grandfather hated Catholics, the bloody RCs, the lying pope, and he blamed them for starting every war, world wars, wars fought before there even were Catholics. And so it made sense that two of his four children—Mary, my mother, and Kathleen—went out and brought home Catholic mates, and a third, Eddie, married a Greek Orthodox woman, which I guess with its priests and pomp and strange tongues was close enough to popery. Only my aunt Mildred married a Protestant. Of course, as people who cross lines do, the three who married these other faiths continued to dislike them. So they wrote another ellipsis into their lives, for themselves.

"Your cousin's marrying a Catholic," my mother says to me darkly, of Nerissa, and I can't help answering, "So did you."

"Your father?" she asks, though his sister Philomena just sent us Mary-shaped bottles of holy water and rosaries from a pilgrimage to Lourdes.

For as long as I can remember the Cassills' center has been Mark, the oldest grandchild, nucleus to their electrons. He was dear dear Mark to my grandmother, just Mark to everyone else, never nicknamed and always consulted, even as a child, on family business. I'm not sure why. The Cassill family worships boys (and I don't use the term out of any love of cliché), and the coming of one as first grandchild, no futzing around with girls, must have been a miracle. Anyway, the family favored him and I can't think of any time when Mark's will didn't hold, though he was a regular boy and is a regular man, a high school art teacher in New Jersey. My grandmother always called him "true Cassill" though he looks just like his Irish father, with a strong curved nose and dark hair.

I asked his mother, my aunt Kathleen, why she'd never had another child and she said that when Mark got old enough to talk she asked him if she should and he said, No.

Mark painted. His work consisted mainly of seascapes and cross sections of ships, with skillful rigging and small, faceless human figures. As a teenager Mark filled out his paintings with quirky touches: a horseshoe crab looming in a corner over a cross-sectioned wreck, or geometrical lines radiating out to swallow up a blank figure.

My parents' New Jersey walls geometric with Mark's paintings, one on top of the other—salt chill licking out in the spaces above the doilies and plaster kittens.

Years later it became a defining moment when Mark like me became crazy for a while, the kind of crazy that's a frank dismissal of all that came before it. It took the Cassills a while to learn to ignore the fact, to erase it, like the dragons at the edge, from their map. It became fashionable thinking in the family that we needed to justify this extreme lapse from the natural order; everyone grew a little dotty, ravaging their minds of reason. He puts so much into his job. He cares too much about his art, he's too gifted.

As a young boy and teenager Mark had become obsessed with Nazism. He never struck me as driven by anti-Semitism, more captivated by the idea of conquest. Down at the shore he played Risk, the game of world domination, obsessively and planned military campaigns all over New Jersey. Perhaps, hearing too many of my grandpa's drowning stories, he reveled in more modern techniques of death. He taught us girls to heil and when I was six forbade us to associate with Jews, an order countermanded by my father, though my father never spoke to Mark about it.

In fact, no one did. I began to realize that my family had for some reason decided never to acknowledge anything that mattered, but to make up for it by relentlessly pursuing the trivial. Everyone—my parents, Mark's parents, my aunts and uncles—focused on Mark's painting. They wondered what kind of watercolors he was using, whether this particular ship was a ketch or a yawl. Eventually Mark left home to go to art school, quit talking about the Third Reich, and got his teaching certificate.

When Mark "broke," as the doctors say, he led his students out of class and marched them through the streets of Paterson, looking for another, mythical school building and probably another life, another New Jersey, another Cassill family, another set of things to corrode his soul. Mark too went into the horizon.

Because even to my grandfather only Mark mattered. Somehow when I think of him telling his Cassill stories I see him talking really to Mark—the only one of us he trusted with his bitterness. Did Mark as a toddler hold his toy men under the water? Did he sit, frozen and solitary, in his child's chair? I just know that somehow my grandpa anointed him the real Cassill grandchild, the one who would carry the family forward, all of them, inside him. Only Mark got Cassill as a middle name, a wedge to divide himself from himself.

And what about me? I was the first girl grandchild, the first fall.

Think of an absurd situation.

You're an actor. You're summoned to the theater: brought. Someone strong pushes you on stage, in your ordinary clothes, the ones that seem to be just you. Other characters mill around, there's a table spread with food, people are talking. I can't describe them except to say that you're struck by their particularity: the food, the clothes, are full of detail and point in some direction, with little touches—the pictures on the walls, the pattern on the china—that suggest a theme. They talk. They have a way of talking. Then everyone looks at you. You have no script. You say something bland, maybe about the decor, and the other characters look uncomfortable. You tell them how you feel and that's worse: disappointment passes like a yawn from face to face. And so it goes, throughout the performance. This is what it means to be born into a family.

Whether my grandpa wrote his script or inherited it, I don't know. I came in at the end.

Because he existed mostly to dislike things—a fulcrum into which ideas or things or people wandered and were expelled—his corner of creation became defined by its exclusions, a kind of ontological vacuum. (The bloody RCs, the damned teetotalers, the snivelers.) The void he made became the space where most of us, his offspring, live. He became in this sense like a god, creating otherness, a separate space for his creatures to exist, safe from the rapacious, making hand. But he was a reluctant god, disgusted by his works, and lacked the godly gift of immortality. He died in his sleep, after mowing the lawn, human.

Because we watched him draw his world out of chaos, or his children did, they learned his physics—creation through erasure, landscape of litter and syncope, where solid things could against all Einsteinian principles disappear. Others have vanished entirely and I, seeing myself through their eyes, see something that grows more transparent every day. So many of us fail.

Louis Charles Harry Clarke Cassill. Two hundred years of Bajan breeding, of genes leaping like flying fish from the material waters—would it be exaggerating to say my grandfather would dislike what his line has come to?

(The bloody RCs, the damned teetotalers, the sniveling ninnies, the suckers, the fools.)

No.

Louis came to the United States from Barbados as an older schoolboy, moving to Brooklyn with his mother—a stunning Creole woman with dark hair and huge heavylidded eyes—and two siblings. His mother went back to Barbados after a while. Louis never did. A relative told me he left Barbados to escape his family—"too crazy," this relative said, "crazy crazy," and pointed to his head. Meaning the real thing: bonkers: and I guess my grandpa hated crazy people too.

Thirteenth of fourteen children, he was occult, broody. His father had died in his seventh year; his mother in a fit of mania killed my grandpa's younger brother by pulling the boy out of his pneumoniac sickbed and forcing him to scrub the kitchen floor, over and over again. At some point my grandpa fled to Canada, maybe to escape her, maybe to escape some trouble with the law. No one knows. We know he cooked in a Canuck logging camp where the loggers eyed him critically each day and said, Cassill, we'd like to kill you if only you'd grow a little and make it interesting. He hated Canadians, the damned peasoupers, beginning then. Almost as much as Catholics, but not quite.

As a married man he claimed Holly Park, on a coast known for pirates, monsters and bankruptcy, in one of his life's few acts of will. He loved the place with a static, secret love, and took in the power plant, the manufacturers that came down after him, as part of the hard landscape he'd chosen.

———

And so for years I wondered what I was supposed to say. And I think Mark must have wondered how he came to be born a god.

Once one of my aunts was watching me. She said suddenly, "You're precocious. Nobody likes precocious children," and picked up a magazine.

This was during the summer, at the shore, where the family's collective spirit respirated through the two small buildings as if they were a set of lungs. We came separately, injected onto the Garden State Parkway in our old Dodge Darts, dripping off at the Toms River exit, sliding above the poisonous plume and beside Denzer & Schafer and finally running together at our end-of-the-road spit where the DDT trucks did their slow and luxurious U-turns and fogged back to Bayville. We came, as my aunt said, to learn to be part of the family.

"It's a man's world, Susie," my aunt Kathleen told me at the shore. My aunt Catherine, Eddie's wife, gathered Helen and me around her there to learn how to do our nails, lose at games, and withhold our opinions. She said, "A woman needs to play her cards right." Then splayed her hands, crabbish, with their ambiguous claws, on the table.

They could have been two of the three fates, or the strophe and antistrophe of a chorus: Kathleen to tell us we'd doomed ourselves by the error of our femininity, Catherine to assure us the fault was remediable, if we acted smart and drew the right man.

My father, with his airline-coffee-colored skin and large nose and black hair, his night-school diploma, never felt accepted by the Cassills, though his insistence on our molding ourselves to the family was absolute.

"You bend over backwards for the family," he said a lot.

"Family is your Rock of Gibraltar," he said. "Everyone else is going to leave you."

My mom has never been one to philosophize like that. She's an extraordinarily small woman with a harsh voice, a voice that says things like, "Your aunt Mildred doesn't think much of you keeping your name." Or, "your grandmother doesn't want you moving to Atlanta."

My grandfather just loomed, *deus ex tenebra.*

"Your grandfather doesn't sleep," my mother told me. My aunts and uncles said, "Your grandfather doesn't sleep." They repeated the fact with lively interest. And in fact he didn't sleep. Still, my grandfather treated his nighttime hours as time irrevocably sworn to some dark god. Night after night he got up from his bed, went to the parlor of whatever house he was in, and sat, with no lights on, staring. For hours. Everyone in the family had funny stories about coming across him, a shape in a dark room, and mistaking him for a burglar or a ghost. It suited him, the near-nonbeing of a man alone in a room he couldn't see, his wife and offspring immobilized by sleep.

"He likes to sit in the dark," my mother concluded.

The order of the grandchildren went like this: Mark; my brother, Chris—my elder by two years—me; Helen; then four more girls. The youngest, Lavinia, was born on Mark's birthday. "A sign," said my aunt Catherine. "No more grandchildren."

After Mark got labeled artistic, Chris became scientific, partly by inclination and partly by default. Girls got catalogued more physically: Helen pert, Melinda dreamy (a ditz, her parents called her), Nerissa bold, Diana emotional, Lavinia spoiled. I tried on most of these parts. Nothing worked: I found myself constantly causing irritation. Over time, in my earlier childhood—six, seven, eight?—it came to me: I had not been given a speaking role.

It seems inevitable. After two boys the Cassill children—three girls and a boy themselves—must have been sure their triple error wouldn't be repeated. And the world had already been divided up, with most of it to Mark and a moiety to Chris. It took them a while to realize there were things they could give girls: things far removed from the mind.

I was given silence. It must have been my grandfather's silence. Mark and Chris got his words and I got that: shaken out, refreshed, refitted. I wore it close to the skin and for the most part only books and my own scribblings joined us. My mother bragged to her siblings that our neighbors thought she had only one child.

As I got older, that silence grew harder to operate, a machine becoming heavier and heavier. I had to have help. This was back in the early seventies, as I started high school in an industrial town in northern New Jersey. A raw balsam odor leaked from the bathrooms; nearby, modeling glue outsold cigarettes.

Marijuana, Carbona cleaning fluid, ups, downs, ludes, hash, acid, heroin. I soon learned that when my own silence ran out more could be taken. There were barbiturate capsules filled with it, slivers of paper soaked with LSD, bags of powdery inwardness. I dropped out of school.

The Cassills tolerated me well enough this way. I roared to the shore house on the back of my boyfriend's Harley, roared out with him at night—waving goodnight behind his ponytail and Peter Fonda stubble—and swayed back in, passing out sometimes before I could find a bed. I felt accepted, even recognized finally (doors left open for me, coffee handed), wearing my silence in an outward, iconic way, a way that could be stumbled over in the night; the Cassills cousins still talk about my druggie years with the air, a friend observes, of people describing an eccentric family pet. My mother, the Cassill in my family and keeper of the family order, treated me with a tightlipped unsurprised irritation. She never hinted I should change.

In fact, it wasn't until I had kicked my drug habit that my grandparents and so my larger family began to erase me, in that wonderful way they had, from the outside in, grudging the small spaces my existence took: my college, my writing, finally resisting if my name came up in a list of Cassills who were tall. My mother and father, who liked me better, kept me almost as a family secret. My brother, a geology student with hair wilder than my dealer boyfriend's, became virtually an only child again.

Now I live far away and have become almost invisible to the Cassills, being also a diagnosed manic-depressive, even before Mark became one—a hubristic move in their eyes, holding as they do that all things related to Mark must be special, capable of becoming myth. I'm not as gone as Helen. She works as a counselor at a clinic and several years ago left the husband her mother selected for her in order to live with one of her patients, a man with thirty-odd personalities, some of them women and children—a polyphony of a man. For this, her mother told me, she's been declared "dead" to the family. She's past tense now, blank space in photographs for the eye to pass over. Not because of the multiple personalities but because she left the man her mother chose, and because her new husband has no job.

Maybe they thought by leaving that silence I destroyed my grandfather somehow, stopped him from continuing. But people with stubborn spirits are harder to destroy than that. No, they're dragged around, like Hector, behind the horse of someone else.

My grandfather left behind on Barbados its coral beaches, where crushed sea creatures glitter like sugar: left the ostentatiously fine weather, the dishes of *coocoo* and callaloo, the Bajan coffins famous for dancing in their tombs. He did it so I can stand here on this gravelly sputumcolored beach, looking out through the light rain of the Northwest, that's been falling for weeks, and has always been falling for weeks. Living in this, the maritime Northwest, feels like living inside an elegy. Quiet but heartfelt. How can he rest?

My grandfather was a man of many citizenships, a Creole in his life and in his blood. He became an American, then a Canadian so he could join the Canadian army and fight in the first world war. Then he reverted to American again. In the army he got shot once, losing several fingers, snuck his name back in the active roster, and got shot again. This time he ended up with a bullet in a cozy conjugal relation with his jugular vein, too close to remove.

He used to point to the slight bulge in his neck where the bullet lodged. "Gives me iron," he said.

The bullet lies in the ground with him now, no doubt outlasting his human tissue. Once, he told us, he noticed a windmill moving the wrong way in the wind. He discovered a Belgian traitor and had him shot. "Monsters," he told us. Of no one in particular.

My family came to Barbados in the 1600s. Or more precisely, my ancestors were brought: they came as indentures or slaves, sold into service due to debt, poverty or—in the case of the Clarkes—as punishment for taking part in a rebellion. The Clarkes had the poor sense to follow the Duke of Monmouth, a dandy who whipped up anti-Catholic fears among some of England's lower classes and led them against the Stuart crown. If they resembled most of Monmouth's followers the Clarkes were poor, hard-drinking, rednecky in an English sort of way and fiercely anti-Catholic. All my ancestors led lives of intense misery, comparable to that of African slaves, in a system of slavery so common that in Britain extracting forced labor was known as "Barbadosing" a man.

Ending an indenture meant signing up for a long term of military service. No doubt many of my ancestors died grotesquely at the hands of the pirates and condemned murderers and lunatics filling up the seventeenth-century Caribbean. Some survived, though, and began like everyone else in the New World the delicate job of recreating themselves, talking their scrubacre into an estate, cyanizing their blood, realizing nothing in that lush unclassified landscape stood ready to contradict them. Bajans always carry on about their aristocratic blood but the truth is that up until the turn of the nineteenth century most of the island stood in foreign hands and most people living on it lived more or less poor. My greatgrandmother, the family's legendary beauty, was just a disturbed woman, constantly abandoning her children, including my grandfather—the man my family invariably referred to, though he talked about eating boiled monkey and pawpaw fruit, as English. With an air of putting the final seal on his propriety.

No doubt my ancestors found Barbados a puzzle, with its two wholly different sides ranged against each other like two possible opinions of the world: the eastern Atlantic side cliffed, unswimmable, a perpetual fury of cold green ocean slapping at a mass of rock; the Caribbean side warm, placid, turquoise, with its famously white, sugary beaches. The island has no twilight either, just the unctuous, glaring sun that finally shuts itself off—click, out!—in favor of deep darkness. Barbados means bipolar, incapable of transition. Here, in this dualistic paradise, my ancestors lost probably half their normal lifespans to typhoid, malaria, or simple overwork.

In the end, I'm grateful to the Cassills, the immediate ones. They have given me the gift of clarity. They've released me. There may be nothing kinder you can do than withhold your love, whatever your reasons, where it's been shown to blight. Inside their circle it's impossible to know anything, to grasp fact, as if somewhere in the line lies an Eve who spat out the fruit of the tree of knowledge once she felt its thrill on the tongue. Her refusal recurs. My family always held that my grandfather was the youngest of thirteen children. They joked about it: the unlucky thirteen, the baker's dozen. When I found out about my grandfather's dead younger brother they said simply, "Oh. Well. Frederick," as if the fact that the boy's name was Frederick implied his existence was always pretty tenuous anyway.

Sometimes when I talk to my mother on the phone she refuses to discuss Helen.

"Mark's painting a little again," she offers instead. "It's better, that thing in his fingers."

"The lithium twitch?" I say. I know she knows what it is; she's seen mine too.

"The thing in his fingers," she says again.

They're like a group of medieval villagers who've found some bizarre map of the cosmos with a flat earth and an ordinary boy in the center and a black plain of things to hate and white wavelets of absorbent quiet, and feel compelled to believe.

Who knows but that they're right in their limits. Maybe their still, divorceless universe of male achievement and female absence feels as safe as the tight teak hull of a ship. Outside there's too much to see— it would be like looking down through the sea itself, watching the bodies spin in their old, doublebreasted sailor's suits.

I have a friend, an older Catholic woman with a pile of hair dyed loud yellow—kind of the shade of fake bananas—and eyelids streaked rosy-purply blue. She once praised our Dungeness crabs to me and added, giggling, "Of course they eat all the dead people under the water," giggling more as her crucifix slid across her sweater.

It's a brazen faith alright, when you can turn your face and hair into monuments to what's not found in nature, when you can imagine the crabs moving over the bodies and still eat.

I often bring my dogs, a retriever and a lame brown-and-white spaniel, to this beach, which is called Little Squalicum. The water's very cold though I see people swimming here in the summer. The beach runs all the way up to the Georgia-Pacific plant, which is dumping mercury and chlorine into Bellingham Bay in order to whiten the toilet tissue it makes.

Once Lum, my spaniel, dragged something large and stinking from a washedup pile of bladderwort—a beheaded seal, probably the victim of a salmon fisherman. The dog rolled his entire body over and over again in the neck wound then ran along the beach, his legs pumping ecstatically as only a crippled dog's can. Typical doggy love of juxtaposition—to be covered in carcass odor and glorying in the living body. We who have no language for death lick at its odor, *memento mori*.

Anyway, the dogs are home today. There are two ways of being at Little Squalicum: the playful way, with dogs and sticks and hunting for beach glass, and the reflective way, absorbing the humped knuckly San Juan islands to the west and the Rockies to the north. Today is the latter, a looking kind of day. I can see up north to Vancouver, Canada, which isn't far from my home. I go there for dinners and movies, so often I have a pass from the Canadian government to cross the border at will. I carry a notepad in my pocket when I come to the beach, remembering as much as I can and writing it down.

Whenever I sit and think my hand tends to wander toward a few-years-old surgical scar, a line that smirks across my lower abdomen. I love the feel of it, like piano wire in my skin, and the way severed nerves have deadened the flesh around it, so it's unable now to tell me what the feel of my fingers is like—touching it feels like touching warm rubber. I can do this: I can enjoy my wounds. In an odd way I enjoy being manic-depressive, as long as it's somewhat controlled. Not like Mark, who backs up to the wall when I see him, hiding his hands, the twitch. I'm the privileged one. Out of an utter silence anything can come.

I had much of each ovary removed. I used to imagine the forward feet of my ancestors stopping short in my womb. I felt guilty, though I am a manic-depressive, after all, from a line of manic-depressives, perhaps, and a former hard-drug user. Maybe those ancestors just wandered off with little philosophical shrugs.

I wonder as I look at the sea if my grandfather's drowned ever drift here—long dead but full of molecular comprehension—idling on the slow roads of the tides. I can see them neaping and flooding north from the noisy Caribbean to the Sound, where, with its cold colorless water and needled unsympathetic trees, they might finally sink. And shut up.

As I sit on a piece of driftwood I can see Lum still, his running ghost or chuffing afterimage, still wearing its manic doggy Marx-brothers smile. He shook on me after rolling in the seal—seawater mixed with bladderwort brine mixed with old blood. A stinking baptism, one of many we get in this life. I think of my own long-ago baptism, and the woody oil of confirmation, that left my forehead pimpled for a week. The Yoruba believe souls pass on into descendants' bodies. I think of the progress of my grandpa's spirit, fallen into the sick, Catholic, almost-Canadian, talky afterlife of my own. Parts of my body have been removed. What does he see, in this gray rainy drugleveled watch? What has he been forced, against the strength of his will, to understand? And the Clarkes, what do they take on the tongue now, world without end, amen? A few lines of an old catechism come back to me—

Is death terrible?
Yes, it is terrible

Chapter Three

Nevertheless, It Moves

The brain looks as if it ought to be a map. Cul-de-sacs and straightaways. All that mazy motion. It's a misleading map, because if you followed its spongiform surface it would circle you randomly around, not even ending where you began. Dante described hell's torments as occurring in folds. This when everyone knew just what brain looked like: a dish to eat on toast and a fat spat out in battle as Dante, a soldier, knew. I don't think the torment of memory is that we have it but that it lies on such inaccessible roads and what we think we know we can never trust.

I'm so afraid I'm mentally ill

I practice my memories. I feel I have to. We Cassills engage so in-stinctively in rewriting ourselves.

There are the blank years of my life. No one, including my parents, will talk about or acknowledge them. No one wants me to talk about them. I am a wrong turn. And from year to year my family changes the pattern of their forgetting: so a few years ago my parents began to say I'd finished high school, though I dropped out as a sophomore. But I like memory; there's something precious about these walks through the wasted landscapes only I can see.

I imagine everyone else in my family taking their own walks through their own frozen spaces, but no one's talking.

My grandmother set this pattern, a woman whose lifework was creating herself and who needed to invent and reinvent the family that reflected her. She made herself up wholesale, a class-switching English-woman, a restless traveler, a Christian Scientist and a genius at spin-ning her own narratives, a talent that began with the narrative of her impregnable immortal body.

My grandmother traded in her mortal body for gossamer, the Christian Science body-as-illusion. Docetism: the belief that the body has no material existence. She lived and preened as a rich woman with no money. She believed she'd founded a dynastic succession of great men. She came to the United States a greengrocer's daughter and became blueblooded, a lover of the crown with Oxbridge accent and Shakespeare on her lips.

She used to say: "You make your own world, you know."

"You know, he never blotted a line, Shakespeare," she also said, which isn't true of him but was of her.

"Shakespeare was a man who understood the human heart," she said, adding, "The man left his wife the secondbest bed."

What she had us remove from our world: my years of drug use, my cousin Mark's psychotic breakdowns, my psychotic breakdowns, my second cousin Mary who moved in with a boyfriend, my mother's uncle Frederick who died at the hands of his mother, my mother's aunt who died at the hands of her mother-in-law. We only believe in nice normal deaths.

Of my cousin Helen, my parents said they have nothing against divorce but she should have asked the family whether she could have one. Then they forgot her.

We forget my father and my uncle's Catholicism and my aunt's Greek Orthodoxy. We forget that my grandfather came from the West Indies and call him British. We forget our multiracial family. We forget manic aunt Rennie who thought her daughter was the Virgin. We forget our thrown-together shore cottages lie on polluted land licked by polluted water. When we reminisce about the gooseberries, droll fruit the color of seasickness, we forget we picked them walking along a chainlink fence guarding a nuclear power plant.

We forget our séances and table possessed by a spirit named Simon. We forget our long stretches of unemployment and delirium.

Or perhaps I'm wrong about all this.

I discovered Frederick, my grandfather's younger brother, by accident in Barbados though he died in the United States. It turned out my mother and her siblings all knew about him. A sulky ghost bloated on neglect. Now he has this much identity: poor Frederick.

"Tell people you and your brother are Episcopalian," my mother always said, though she's a former Christian Scientist and my father's Catholic. She told me to tell people we had summer houses and were half British and my father had a desk job. Which we had and we were on a technicality and he did.

————————

As far back as I can remember, when I've learned a fact about the family, like poor Frederick's story, I rehearse it to myself. I say to myself what I've heard and I repeat it over and over, maybe write it down. I'm terrified of forgetting. I know if I ask about Frederick again I'll hear a different version of the truth, that I've been offered a shape for the past that'll never come my way again. I know too what I memorize may be false but I'm resolved that my reality should at least be the first one I hear about.

My brother has no memories before the age of ten. My family doesn't speak of me much. It makes me wonder if I still exist or if I too have slipped off. Or my brother was invented to replace me.

My mother, the oldest Cassill child, looks exactly like my aunt Kathleen, the youngest: same sharp features and beige wavy hair and oblong jaw. My husband used to confuse them. Between them lie another sister and a brother. We share birthdays.

My mother and father called us *Chrisuse! Chrisuse!*

My family has many redundancies.

For creating such an Etch-A-Sketch family, my grandfather and grandmother were extraordinarily suited. In many ways they never meshed but in this way they did: my grandfather provided the vacuum, the absences, and my grandmother the fantasy, fillings for his gaps. Almost everything in the world disgusted my grandfather, where my grandmother had her own world that delighted her to no end.

"It's a good address, Fanwood," she said a lot of the town where she lived, though it's a drone of a suburb, boxy and boring as a Monopoly set, a commuter town like thousands in New Jersey. Her previous town, Westfield, had also been a good address.

"Dear Mrs. Swenson" did my grandmother's hair and other dear misters and missuses supplied her needs for meat and groceries and new plumbing, people who seemed so intimate yet so fleet in their duties you'd have thought they appeared from a servants' wing.

"And how is your lady mother?" my grandmother asked when I visited.

At meals she said things like, "I believe I shall dillydally with some brussels sprouts. Should you like to dillydally with some brussels sprouts?"

She managed to make such statements sound, if not natural, at least like she wasn't surprised to hear herself. I described her accent as Oxbridge but that's somewhat inaccurate as the truth is I've never heard another accent like it and doubt it exists or ever did in any real place.

"Who do you think you are," she grinned. "That's who you are, you know."

At the shore she padded over the slanted, ancient green linoleum discolored by rust. She always seemed to be looking for a little girl, to send out for rose hips or wild strawberries or hot water.

She laughed, "Louie does so like roughing it."

It was my grandmother's conceit to call our place Holly Park. Most people used the name Bayville. The fantasy—tony people leaning their workfrazzled faces to the breeze—jumped from the developer's head into hers. Our house (with its heatless peagreen sagging) wasn't really part of the Holly Park subdivision. Anyway, there wasn't a Holly Park. It jumped out a Wall Street window in 1929.

My grandmother had copies of masterpieces by Rembrandt on her wall, each illuminated like a museum piece by its own oblong light. Like all the Cassills she kept her rooms dark. I remember her heavy parlor with the indistinct shapes of her offspring scattered around, above them the well-lit faces of her copies in their lozenges of light. I remember especially Rembrandt's *Head of a Child*.

"Do you see the strokes Susie? A poet with the brush."

She loved cats and said of hers, "Dusty is a gentleman cat, you see he always leaves a bit in his bowl. He doesn't gobble up like a ruffian."

She found and cooked in the middle of New Jersey things like mutton chops and mint sauce. Several times at Christmas she made a plum pudding and brought it to the table in flames, a fat torch burning blue with a wide halo, a burning bush springing from her middle.

Once we arrived at her house for dinner and found the table bijouxed with cloth napkins—the timelessly elegant triangle fold—a tablecloth, candles in silver holders and a TV dinner set squarely at each place setting.

"I do so think Swanson is lovely," my grandmother said.

My mother humbly tucked into her food. My father said, "Jeez." My brother and I sighed in ecstasy.

My grandfather Louis sold insurance; I don't think he graduated from high school. My grandmother had worked as a nurse in World War I, which means someone trained her by giving her a wad of bandages and shoving her at a patient. She didn't have much education either but quoted her Shakespeare and played scratchy recordings of Caruso. She lived at her good address and raised lady mothers and objected violently to my father and my uncle Joe as in-laws, because my uncle had only a seventh-grade education and my father's father, fourth grade. Their families were immigrants, Catholics, poor. My grandmother's children resisted her in choice of spouses though in my mother's case she went on to make my father ashamed of all the things that had made him a good contrarian choice. She refused to eat Italian food, cooking it because my father insisted, and then sitting at the table eating cold peas in mayonnaise.

———

My grandmother, like my grandfather, was small. I don't know what she looked like as a young woman but the older woman I remember had very ordinary features, eyes of an unemphatic blue: the sky as it washes out when it meets the ocean. Her nose and mouth were small and regular in a rounded face. By sixty she had a pronounced dowager's hump, the result of her low calcium intake or a knot in her consciousness.

I remember even as a young child finding her charming, and her charm lay in things other than the physical. She had a beautiful voice. Her accent shaped each phrase out like a beautiful balloon.

"Such a pity the art of conversation is dying," she said a lot. She knew where her strengths lay.

I loved my grandmother though I never believed she loved me or any of her grandchildren except the two boys: even that resembled love less than an author's dreaming for her protagonists. The Cassills always thought of girls not as bad but as kind of pointless. Future wives and housekeepers, lures who might bring more interesting men into the family. My mother believes women do not have the capacity for brains men have, a fact she can go on about for ages and claims has been printed in the *New York Times*. We're not even much good at producing boys.

I once shocked my mother by telling her most couples who adopt state a preference for a girl. She said, "But why would anyone *want* a girl?" A blunt old lady now, my mother, though the question seemed genuinely troubling to her and not rhetorical, as if such a thing might reveal a flaw in her cosmology, something she hadn't thought about.

My grandmother too held to these beliefs about women. She felt certain she'd transcended her body but believed it was a transcendence permitted to few.

Grandma is nice. She calls me "Niobe," whoever that is. (6/9/68, age 11)

Loving my grandmother as I did and as we all did was a proving ground, a spiritual exercise, like something young monks should have to do. Loving her spun around her inability to love back. Her self-centeredness—her image of herself as a celestial body revolving brilliantly in a cold space—formed not a side effect but a basis of loving her. Ours was a love real and helpless and hard as birth. Like learning to love the world, something that can only regard you sideways and with a kind of amusement.

When my grandmother died my aunt Kathleen said a few days later that she already missed her and it came out with a lot of anger, the voice of the powerless and enmeshed.

For her children my grandmother's inability to love hurt, I'm sure, and led to four bitter natures, a divided and hostile attitude toward life itself, as if things always stood ready to take something from them. For me my grandmother's unlovingness had a comfort about it. I don't recall sitting in her lap or anything but I remember folding up near her as if I were sitting in a book; it felt that way. I loved her the way I loved a story and something about her always reminded me of paper, her fragile inky skin, her dryness and papery moulting.

This evening I went over my grandmother's house. She is a lot of fun. She has some of the funniest stories, about when she was out traveling in other countries. (6/25/69, age 12)

My grandmother traveled compulsively. It gave her a great repertoire. She told stories to us, her grandchildren, without censorship. When she went to Amsterdam, she told us, she had almost nothing to spend so she went to the cheapest place in the city and it turned out to be a brothel.

"I wondered why the other guests were so restless," she said, "and that funny light over the door."

While she talked my grandmother clattered a cup of tea in a teacup with a saucer. She drank Lipton's. The Lipton man smirked at us under his moustache.

She told us how during the war someone offered her a cigarette treated with opium and she smoked it, feeling the world dim out—"It was really quite lovely," she commented sadly.

And of course she told us about Christian Science.

"Why would a good God create sickness and death? He wouldn't," and she looked round at us face by face. "Do you believe God would want to hurt you?"

Then she added the inscrutable, "Jesus was a metaphysician, you know."

She called us girl grandchildren *Pretty pretties*. It was entirely immaterial to her what we did.

It's the late 1990s now. My grandmother's granddaughters are mostly infertile. Running out of Pretty pretties. I have an enormous tumor in my throat, a toxic adenoma. The doctors I have been seeing about it— various doctors because I move around a lot—ask questions about radiation. Did I have it as a child for acne? Tonsillitis? Can I prove that I didn't? I'm sure this theory is wrong but I call my mother anyway, who sputters in horror.

"Doctors treat things with radiation?" she asks, good quasi– Christian Scientist that she is.

I call someone I know at the New Jersey Department of Environmental Protection, to ask about the power plant and BOMARC. His name is Gerry and he's always pleasant and full of alternatives.

"Did you know when you were born they took babies away from their mothers and bombarded their necks with radiation if their thymus gland looked large?" he says helpfully. "I know it's hard to believe but that was standard practice."

I say my parents wouldn't have given permission and he says nobody asked permission, they just did it. "Only took a minute."

Wasn't that bad? Oh, it was terrible.

Gerry fills me in a little on cholinesterase inhibitors, pesticides that screw up brain chemistry, just as an afterthought.

So now Ocean County's famous, not for its lady mothers but for its disease clusters. Downtown Toms River has a large, simple (in the mode of the Vietnam Memorial) pink-and-cream monument to the children who've died of cancer. Thirty-two names have been chiseled onto it and more wait to be added. And there's the breast cancer and lung cancer and leukemia. Berkeley and Brick Townships have their clusters of autism, children born with the soul of my grandfather, untouchable and still.

I want to contact my grandmother, May (I think of her as a person now), in the ether and find out what she and Mary Baker Eddy think about this, if praying over us, if *thinking* basically is enough when your porous body gets spattered with nuclear isotopes and toxic chemicals. Have the rules changed.

It's easy to see that the Ciba-Geigy people and Denzer & Schafer people and Nick Agricola were themselves Christian Scientists, believers in the docetic body. They poured sludges in the ground we drank from and the river we swam in, thinking we lived in two different dimensions. I love my grandmother's religion: I believe it in a way and yet I believe I'm sick. Maybe we did live bodiless. Maybe by treating ourselves as impregnable we've somehow renounced the privilege, incarnating ourselves slowly into the world we've fouled.

Like my grandfather's, my grandmother's life story as handed down by her and her children has holes and often makes little sense. Born May Radford, she grew up as one of eight children in a small village in Lincolnshire, England. Her father sold fresh vegetables from a stand.

She rarely mentioned her parents though she once told me her father was a radical Whig who'd burned down the house of a Tory. In World War I May got taught to cut and patch, and nursed the wounds of men shipped home from the front. One of them was my grandfather Louis, though he was either an American or Canadian citizen at the time.

While nursing she embraced Christian Science.

"The war converted her, the butchery," my mother says. "You know, they just chopped everything off."

She spoke from her mother's memories but didn't elaborate. I know doctors then loved amputation. So my grandma embraced the doctrine that the body could not be ill but only the spirit controlling it, the spirit that in fact made up the body. Matter as error. The belief in prayer as the only healing because the body's false, and wounds are just spiritual waywardness. It's hard to imagine such a faith blooming in a ward full of men shaking with fever, leg stumps and arm stumps and the stench of gangrene. My grandfather, her patient, lost two very human fingers to a sniper in that war.

In every family story there's a detail that provides, if you notice it, the key. In the case of my grandmother's conversion to Christian Science the key to her character is that she kept on nursing. Believing she did no good, that her job involved something like sin, not to herself but to her patients, she dispensed ether and codeine and assisted in surgeries, holding lopped-off feet or shins or hands afterward though she had by then the docetic belief that such bloody detritus were illusion. When I thought about this recently I thought about her in later life, her inscrutability.

She said, "If only you knew the Universal Mind."

She raised her four children Christian Scientist, though she seemed philosophical about it when they left the church: as if she'd known all along they wouldn't understand. My grandma lectured me about her faith and from time to time threw away my medicines, antibiotics and such; she amused us by bringing up Christian Science all the time and tailoring it to the person she was speaking to.

When I was twenty-five and making good decisions for a change I married my husband, Bruce, a poet, and she said, "It's the poetic religion, you see," whenever she saw him.

"It's the scientific religion," she said to my brother, a geologist.

All with the air of a prophet speaking to the townsfolk of Gomorrah. She would have been shocked and I think a little dismayed if any of us had followed her. It was her own body she saw revolving in its untouchable glow, on the spiritual plane.

In fact my grandmother left her children in a limbo where their bodies didn't glow but sagged and cramped, and still could not be healed. Or not without deep shame and the healing of one member becoming the cleft and stigma of another. My mother once got a false diagnosis of breast cancer and told no one. She didn't even tell my father about her doctor's appointments. I don't know if she thought she could go away for a few days and slip back into the house breastless, her body showing the scars of her spirit's failure. When I had a miscarriage and surgery a few years ago my mother got so flustered when I called she just handed the phone to my father.

My mother let slip once that she'd remained a Christian Scientist until her late twenties; she wouldn't say more. She says her mother did not take her to doctors that she can recall. She can't remember her mother performing the Christian Science prayer healings over her either, though she thinks that must have happened sometimes. My mother's not resentful of this lack of medical care, she says. She can't remember being sick. She can't remember me being sick as a child either, and adds when I cried at night, night after night, she locked my crib in the bathroom of the apartment and closed her own door to drown me out.

———

My grandmother drank gin and wine and caffeinated tea every day, though all these things are strictly off limits to Christian Scientists. My uncle Eddie used to ask her how she lived with herself but she just grinned. She remained convinced that Mary Baker Eddy had been off on a few points.

My grandmother ruled us until her death, not just what we did but how we thought about things. She vetoed grandchildren's names and set dates for weddings and monitored holiday and summer plans. Like a press agent she created an instant response, a handling, to family trouble. My father bitched about spending summer weekends and holidays with the Cassills rather than his own family but nevertheless loaded coolers in the car as if he had no choice, like something caught by gravity.

My visits home still feel like submitting to the physical rules of another order. I think of Galileo when he sat before the Inquisition of 1633. This isn't a grandiose comparison: Galileo was a coward, and so am I. Under threat of torture he knelt, a feeble old man in a gown of sackcloth, and took back his belief in the Copernican system, a heliocentric solar system in which the earth revolves around the sun. Galileo had designed and built his own telescopes and seen for himself evidence of the earth's orbit. Unfortunately the church had declared war on Copernican astronomy. An earth that's not the center of things might imply that humans, God's image, might not be the center of things. Galileo resisted just a little. Then he assured the tribunal of his belief in a fixed earth, put there by God so no one would ever wonder which planet really mattered.

Once when I called my mother with some questions about our well she put the phone down and said, "Nick! She's asking about the water again."

She responds to my stories about Ocean County contamination by saying, "We're all still here, aren't we?"

So I've quit talking about the groundwater and radiation and DDT. When I go home to New Jersey I try to find out secrets, but sneakily. I play the good child. I don't argue and I censor myself, avoiding the subjects of high school or mental illness or drugs.

I might say, "How's your garden? My snowdrops are up."

Or, "How's Giuliani doing? What smells so good? Can I make dinner?"

I work in references to forbidden subjects like Helen once in a while but innocently, as if I've forgotten I'm forgetting them.

Even my dad uses the term "the family" to mean the Cassills, and he too uses it to mean one overwhelming thing. He's a bit more Brooklyn-y than the others: "That's shitting all over the family," he says a lot.

Writing this would be shitting all over the family.

With the Cassills mates are chosen partly for their porous qualities, so they can absorb the family version of things, the family way of doing things: to observe boundaries, no matter how mad they get.

Once a year my dad checks in on me by asking Bruce, "Do those pills still work?"

It made sense to me that my grandmother's faith sprang from a religion founded by another great matriarch, whose words place next to Christ's at services. Mary Baker Eddy, like my grandmother, grew disgusted with the medicine of her day and founded a church that was also a philosophy. My grandmother grew disgusted with medicine and founded a family that was also a philosophy. Her foundational faith lay in the solubility of the past to the acids of desire.

My grandmother once told me, when I was a teenager, that she took my grandfather's ring casually after a few dates in London; since she'd accepted him her mother forced her into the marriage as a matter of principle.

"I was foolish," my grandmother said.

When my grandfather died fifty-odd years later my grandmother arranged a Christian Science memorial service though throughout their life together he'd asked her, and she'd promised, not to. She sat through the readings of Mary Baker Eddy with an inexpressibly soft play of approval on her lips. She never seemed dismayed by his death though she'd woken up one morning to find him dead in bed, quite natural under the chenille, heart failure at eighty-eight after a normal day of mowing the lawn and such. I don't know how soon she called her children. She didn't cry and expressed no sorrow but invited her family over to finish the jugs of Manhattans my grandfather kept under their sink.

"Louie wouldn't have wanted me to cry," she said, hoisting her drink.

Whatever he wanted my grandmother sat at the service with the soft ray playing across her mouth. I do know she loved having the house to herself. She let it be known a few days later that no one would pass the night in her house again.

In my earliest childhood my grandmother lived in Westfield, New Jersey, in a large old house her adult children moved in and out of, when single and with spouses and children too. I remember it vaguely as an old rambling place with lavender-skirted vanity tables and lots of pilly chenille.

My mother lived at the Westfield house until her marriage at age thirty-three and she and my father lived there several times after their marriage, including some time with my brother Chris. My aunt Kathleen and uncle Joe lived there with my cousin Mark and so did my aunt Catherine and uncle Eddie with their daughter Helen, and my aunt Mildred until she married at close to forty. All of the generation before mine in the family lived there and all talked about their time there obsessively, the in-laws at least, like veterans reminiscing about Hamburger Hill. My grandmother accused my father of being vulgar and my mother of being dull. She told my aunt Catherine she had no idea how to take care of Eddie and belittled their child. She offered her comments to the air, as if Universal Mind shared her disgust at her children.

"Mary certainly has dampened the party," she would say to the air, or "The party is turning vulgar."

She liked to talk about the toll people were taking on a party no one but she knew was taking place. Nevertheless she insisted her children and spouses and even their children move in with her and they complied. They did pretty much whatever she told them to do. She had my mother set her wedding on a day that she was menstruating so her marriage wouldn't be consummated, whether accidentally or on purpose I don't know. My father took it as a strike at him and railed about it for the rest of his life.

After the Inquisition Galileo did dare to hang on to his manuscripts of the heavens' movements, his sketches for telescopes; he held them secretly and his good Catholic wife passed them on to her confessor when Galileo died and the good priest burned them. Galileo's observations are great and mine are small but I do keep mine anyway, and you could call this my act of resistance. But it's a weak act, weaker than kneeling and lying. I've used five or six different pseudonyms in my life. The name I'm using now is not my name but the name of a recovered female relative, a lost woman, and as a recovered woman she's just a skeleton that must be fleshed out by the same process of fantasizing and filling in that I resist. My life has had four or five very discrete chunks and depending on which ones I speak about I become a different person. I'm more like my grandmother than any of her other offspring but this fact holds not delicious irony but sad farce.

And the more I remember the more I doubt my memory. No one will answer my questions, so I can be at most the voice of entropy, of history breaking up. This is the fleshing in of a woman's body. I can give you my diseases but not my name.

My family legacy happened in the body. The two boys held the gifts of the mind. My grandmother believed Mark was a great painter and my brother would be a great scientist. At family gatherings she said, "Dear dear Mark. Mark will leave the world something." And she said, "I believe the future of the oceans is safe in Chris's hands."

My cousin Mark went on to break down, though my grandmother never acknowledged that. My brother became a geologist and shunted the oceans onto someone else.

She never paid much attention to the girls, my writing or our various jobs and marriages. I never sensed she remembered what I did or my cousins did. If she'd been alive when my cousin Helen divorced she would have participated in the shunning of her, though, a slow ruminative spitting out where the family recounted anecdotes with Helen's part left out. I was in my thirties then and made it a point to ask my mother about Helen once in a while, for practice. She said "Who?" in genuine wonder.

When my cousin Mark broke my aunt Kathleen visited him in a mental ward. The cops had picked him up, wandering around with his students. He tore the first hospital room they put him in to pieces. My grandmother said, "Poor Mark. He takes his job too seriously."

My aunts and uncles took up her position: he's fine, he just takes his job too seriously. Only my aunt Kathleen said, "There's something terribly wrong with him, and it's something wrong in all of us." She brought the thought up from deep within like a sibyl and used that preposition, "in," not "with." She said, "Mother lives in a fantasy world and we all do." Then she lapsed back into the family's peculiar silence.

In fact, Mark's manic-depressive and so am I and so certainly was my greatgrandmother and maybe my grandfather, who had something wrong with him. My family hasn't paid much attention to my disease. No one's ever visited me in the hospital or made reference to my illness. Mark's hospitalizations mattered because they needed to be glossed somehow, like the inscrutable words of a desert prophet.

When Mark's breakdowns found a reason, though, they were also soon forgotten. Once at dinner my cousin and I talked about connections between mental illnesses and the visual arts, manic-depressive painters and poets, when my parents interrupted and said, "That's ridiculous. Look at Mark. *He's* a painter."

The year before Mark had spent four months in a mental hospital. I'd been in one a few years before that. At the time Mark and I had identical palsies in our hands from lithium (it turned out I only respond to a drug used to treat seizure disorders and autism) and chronic knee thrusts from haldol. Our eyes purged with moisture. Our faces bloated, another side effect. We looked like two ancient beings strapped into young skins. When we reminded my parents of Mark's manic-depression they got the blank disconcerted Cassill look, like priests who've performed a bad exorcism.

At the shore we used to play Scrabble endlessly, especially during the rain; we had only a few electric lights and these went out during storms, so we used kerosene for light, those pearshaped glass lamps that throw thick smokey circles on the walls. In these we hunched over our letters. Except for the children the family sat together in silence as often as not. We kids were pretty still as kids go. We sat around a card table on hard chairs, with just the rain sounds and the clacking of the Scrabble tiles, as everyone arranged and rearranged their letters.

I always picture us this way: the lightness of the Scrabble tiles, the four heads (we always played in fours) frowning over the wiggliness of language. *Need* is *eden* and *pear* may *rape* and *reap* itself. If it's a *rood* it's a *door*. Someone puts down a *mist* and it becomes *pessimist* soon. An *ill* becomes a *will*. My family played wicked games of Scrabble.

My grandmother's heroine, Mary Baker Eddy, married three times and had one son. She didn't raise, or have much to do with, her son. It's hard to figure out why from the hagiographic accounts of her life. One calls him "a handful" and says her father took him away from the young widow to be raised by a couple, who then moved off to Minnesota. She doesn't seem to have done much to keep up.

My grandmother must have identified with this story—with Mary Baker's ultimately solo quest for her own wholeness. Her husband my grandfather was an abandoned child and she herself left her family often. She traveled in a way that felt what we'd now call *addicted,* going to England for months, Barbados, Europe, all over the world. She had no money but got steerage tickets, rooms in brothels, steamer deals. At seventy-nine she went on safari to Africa and slept in the tops of trees, above the Masai. All the cousins were teenage by then, gaga over her stories of how the Masai live off the blood of their cattle; they open the jugular vein with a practiced jab, she told us, put a bowl to it and seal the wound when the bowl fills brimming.

I don't know how much time she spent away from home when my

mother was little. A lot, I gather, but I'm not sure. I can't imagine any-one being left in the care of my still, brooding, melancholic grandfather.

"Your aunt Kathleen really resented Mom's leaving," my mother told me once. I asked her to tell me more. She said uneasily, "You know. She just thought Mom should have stuck around."

When I asked my mother if she resented my grandmother's traveling she shrugged and answered, "Oh I don't know."

I guess it's inevitable that when my grandmother got old and senile her four children repressed that fact too, and she stayed alone much longer than she should have. They resented caring for her at the end, and had fights and hung up on each other. My uncle Eddie, a blunt man who models himself on Winston Churchill ("Winnie"), wanted to bung her, as he put it, right into a nursing home. My aunt Mildred, whom my grandmother always went easy on, yelled at everybody to do more but didn't come. Aunt Kathleen, the honest one, was most tender and my mother most bitter.

The fact is, my grandma grew hard to care for, cantankerous, nasty, crazy. Her children hired homecare women and my grandma chased them out of her house. Christian Science teaches that a perfect under-standing of its doctrine leads to immortality, not a misty Other Side but a clear self that's born (however a spirit can be born) into this world in its illusory but able-to-eat-a-grape form and never dies. When she started to die my grandmother got palpably pissed. She looked like Lear in her house, striding around, hair sticking up, old filthy nightie on and quilted bathrobe unpinned. You'd think Mary Baker Eddy's death would have taught her something.

Her memory went with those occasional wholenesses that pop up like figures in a children's book: she recited Shakespeare's Sonnet 116 obsessively, long after she'd forgotten most of her family. When my mother and aunts took her to her annual Resident Alien registration she had no idea what to do and said "Let me not to the marriage of true minds admit impediment" over and over to the clerk. Somewhere in the cortical folds where the neuroelectric pathways have burned out a few cells stay lit—why, I wonder? Do these mean something? Or is the stuff of the body, which has its own sense of irony, asserting itself at last?

As for the Poetic Religion, the Scientific Religion—as soon as my grandmother felt something wrong with her heart her docetism staggered and she asked to be taken to a doctor. She gained that much mental clarity, to know her heart was failing and panic. There wasn't much the doctor could do, so in this sense Mary Baker Eddy proved right. My grandmother broke with her Christian Science group for a while and then we started finding them at her house again, a group of older women all in a circle, praying for the healing of the uncomprehending Learlike woman in their midst.

It was terrible to see someone so afraid to die. There were no platitudes—a life well lived, dying surrounded by a healthy family, being remembered—that could encircle the enormity of her fear. Our presence offered her nothing. We could have been winked out of existence for all she cared. She grew haggard with her fear, her jowls and ribs shrinking, her eyes wild and distracted. She'd lost the charming carelessness of the woman in love with her solitude.

My grandmother died haunted. I don't mean just by her death. She saw ghosts and phantoms every night when she went to bed, hiding in her room and pouring in through the windows. They made her scream. She lived in a world of bad spirits. I'd moved far away by then so I don't have my grandmother's descriptions of them, just my mother's laconic ones: "Oh, you know. Bad."

For my grandmother's spirits I imagine red eyes, fangs, batwings, sly little grins. But who knows. They may have been dead soldiers from the first world war, Tories burned by her father, or the winged soul of Mary Baker Eddy herself, a staunch woman with a Temperance set to her lip.

My grandmother died at ninety of heart failure, just before my family made the final move of transferring her by ambulance to a nursing home. It was peaceful. She had gotten into the hospital somehow, where she just died, and we buried her and she went on to irritate my aunt Kathleen by making my aunt miss her.

I miss her too. I miss her benign look and her oblivious optimism. Even her terrible cooking, everything boiled or baked past the point of belonging to the organic universe. And to know what lay in her head, what she mapped, has disappeared. It's knowing that things I want to know are gone and the false beautiful land, the one that spun and spun around in her brain and went nowhere, is gone too.

Galileo had one moment of rebellion, an old man in his old man's skin, kneeling in sackcloth before the inquisitors. He did not want to anger them. A Pisan, a Tuscan, he liked his long Tuscan meals of lamb and organ meats, his walks by the lopping wedding cake of a tower. He was not brave in the sense of the many Renaissance figures, like Savonarola, who defied church authority under torture. But as he rose from his knees before the inquisitors, after recanting his beliefs in a revolving earth, he muttered, *"Eppure, si muove"*—"Nevertheless, it moves." He wasted one last piece of breath affirming his eyes. No one knows who he spoke to, the recanting man next to him, or just himself. And the tone—a statement? A question? Then Galileo went on to live his life with his meals and his notebooks. And it does move, I think. But I can't see it and I'm not sure.

Chapter Four

The Running Feet

We're here. No, here. No (the screendoor shuts like a page turning), over here.

Knocking ourselves from light to light, veering at the candle. Giddy and very serious about it. The air's dark and rich with fireflies' here-and-there firepricks and the darker zags of mosquitoes. My aunt Catherine sits against a window inside the house smoking and her cigarette glows up and down through the air, elegant regular movements, like she's teaching the fireflies how to do it. I can just see her ash; it builds to a crumbling thumbnail before she taps it off. She's one of those smokers with an uncanny sense of how far she can trust her cigarette. She gets her hair dyed, teased and shellacked once a month and it clouds on her head like the calm center of a squall. She's half in, half out. She brought baklava and meatballs with mint. My grandmother refused them.

Behind her my grandfather rocks in a corner, doing his statue routine. It's not so much that he stares at the wallpaper as that the air of scrutiny belongs mainly to the wallpaper, looking at him.

Next to him on the old couch my grandmother plays dowager empress. She's talking and talking and I can only hear her knowing tone, which is all that anyone's meant to hear.

Mark's brought down a stereo and he put it in the larger of the Little Bungalow bedrooms and has cranked up The Doors. Periodically he runs in to jam his head between the two speakers, which he squeezes against his ears with the volume way up. He does this for "Soul Kitchen," "Strange Days" and "The End"

Of our elaborate plans the end
Of everything that stands the end
No safety or surprise the end

Because this is Mark's favorite song and because it's morbid and because it's emotional and dissonant we all love it. We know the lyrics to it and most all Doors songs by heart, and we scream them out together, in our yard and on the Bayville Road, in the rich fruitcake dark.

This is the end beautiful friend
It hurts to set you free
But you'll never follow me

Anyway, let's say nothing out of the ordinary is happening. Mark's run in to listen to "The End" and we're having an argument.

Chris says really soon. Helen and I say fifteen years. Mark thinks ten and runs to hear The Doors sing about it. We're trying to decide among ourselves how much longer the world will last.

"That's stupid," Chris says. "World War II was twenty years after World War I, so we're *late*. It's going to be anytime. We'll just get bombed and then we'll have to bomb back. Bombs are automatic now anyway."

We think about this. I don't know much that's automatic—remember, we're just beyond manual typewriters—so I imagine the pieces of pie dropping into their slots at the Horn & Hardart's Automat in New York. You take one, quivering with too much meringue, another identical one falls down.

Helen says, "Everybody has the A-bomb. Or the H-bomb." She's ten and has no clue what these distinctions mean, but in our generation everybody places an initial before the bomb. We kids are very quick with these rhetorics that show mature understanding—we say *Red China, Broadway play, wall-to-wall carpet.*

Mark comes back and says Germany's going to get back together, then forget it.

Helen and I opt for Indochina or one of the oil-rich countries like Saudi Arabia which, we remind him, probably also have the A-bomb and the H-bomb or could get them.

"You know, the first one's heading for New York," Mark says. "New Jersey's going to shrivel away."

Boys in my area always say this. We've been doing air-raid drills since grammar school, taught to march single file to the basement and crouch down with our coats over our heads or nestle under our desks with our coats over our heads. Our mothers sigh and scrawl our names into white bands on our clothes and there's an unspoken knowing that all this naming will help ID our remains. Boys, who seem to feel they have to do this sort of thing, whispering that New York's going to be the first to go and us with it, without even the dignity of being a primary target. This last irritates me, and I find myself arguing there's plenty in New Jersey worth blowing up.

The end of the world is our theme, like my grandmother's Shakespeare and my aunt's cigarettes and my grandfather's silences. We're very very cheerful kids, in the manner of people who know their problems will soon be decisively ended.

Because it's 1969 we put on The Doors' latest album, *Soft Parade*, next, though we all agree it's not as good as the others. Jim Morrison screeches a lot and his voice holds the fret of the mosquitoes. Because it's 1969 the nuclear reactor's just opened and the air's newly full of radioactive particles, freed from their few minutes in holding tank purgatory, looking for their rest. There's strontium-90, which ends up in the bones, and tritium, which becomes part of the body's water. Iodine-131, heading for the thyroid. Ordinary plants have been known to make weird extravagant mutations near nuclear reactors: at one reactor in Sellafield, England, a white flower changed to blood red.

If we'd known this about reactors we would have been ecstatic, searching the fields and the marshes on our hands and knees.

A local woman who has leukemia told me she heard the Kirkwood-Cohansey aquifer wanders across the country and its path is visible aboveground in a long lazy river of mutated creatures: legless frogs and sexless trout, blind muskrat, pinkeyed birds. She kept calling it the "aquifilter." It's a beautiful fiction, all the links in the chain of being united by a snake of water, like her name for it is a beautiful fiction. My mother calls it the Kennedy aquifer, a Camelot underground.

If it's twilight, which I guess it is with all these bugs, my uncle Joe and my father will come out to "stretch their legs." They're always stretching their legs, walking slowly over to the pier, speculating on tomorrow's weather, moseying down the street. My grandmother will come ask us to play Occupations, which none of us want to do, because she cheats shamelessly, using jobs like ostler, jobs that haven't existed since she was a young girl in England.

We're bored before my grandmother comes. We figured out World War III long ago. Playing with her, making wild guesses at impossible anachronistic things, we're even more bored and want to go back to the old boredom.

Everyone in my family is always bored. If we're here we want to be there. My second cousin Mary calls it having itchy feet but what do feet have to do with it? Unless we've gotten that old West Indian curse of the running feet, cayenne pepper sprinkled into your footsteps so you can never stay still.

Or starting as a family of exiles we got used to the idea of exile, maybe even to like it, because we always exile ourselves and one another. And we remember the island, the first exile—Barbados, a little cliffy place between two oceans, each water held up to us like a cup.

I am forty and as an adult have never lived anywhere longer than five years. Now I live about as far as I can from my native New Jersey without a change of citizenship: northwest Washington where the sea eats the sun at night instead of spitting it out in the morning. My brother too can't stay, living in Minnesota but leaving for months at a time. He gives papers in South Africa and Australia and takes short-term teaching jobs in Japan and Italy. We live as if life is a temporary thing, or as if we're outrunning the International Date Line.

Still, everywhere we go we're terrible creatures of habit, calling home on Sunday, searching out cold cereal and chocolate milk.

Here's a story I got out of my aunt, my father's sister.

My father's grandfather came to New Jersey from southern Italy, a middle-aged man, to work for a little while. Lots of men in his village were doing this, getting on in factories and shipyards and sending back a little of the cash no one had at home. His village, sixty miles above Naples and isolated at the top of a mountain, was (is) scorchingly poor and ravaged all the time by earthquakes and disease. He got work in the United States but soon got word that his wife and children had died back home in an epidemic of cholera. How that news must have felt to him I can't imagine: like the end of the world. He had five children; they and his wife lived in a tiny one-room cottage, where the goats and chickens stayed too if the weather was bad. My greatgrandfather did not go back. He did not change his way of relating to the United States, continuing to keep to himself and avoid English, acting temporary. Then he sat down one day and wrote a careful letter to his wife's best friend, a woman whose surname was Antonetta, back in Gesualdo. He asked her to get passage on a boat to this country and marry him and allow him to have more children. I know a lot about him—that he was a stern man, that he loved cats, that when he died his cat sat by his corpse in the living room, then vanished—but I don't know anything about his wife. No one telling the story, my father or his father or his sister, seems to find her behavior strange. Why did she go, I wonder. What did she leave, that this seemed better?

From what I hear my greatgrandfather's second wife looked like the first, acted like her, cooked the same dishes and had the inscrutable dialect of his dead wife's village. In middle age he had another family, six children this time.

I don't know much about his life in the United States. I know at one point he had a tiny rowhouse in Brooklyn and lost it somehow, and got himself a piece of land in the rural town of Bound Brook, New Jersey, where he built himself another rowhouse, brick by brick, narrow, rectangular and elongated, with narrow rooms whose walls squeezed in from the pressure of the other rowhouses which were of course not there.

My greatgrandfather lost the Bound Brook house too. It still exists, in the town where Union Carbide would make its Bic pen plastic and pour the dregs into metal drums headed for Reich Farm.

People pull up and stare at my greatgrandfather's house because it speaks so crudely of city streets, an Italian neighborhood, animated talks on the stoop and vegetable stands on the corner. They wonder how it got there. They can maybe hear my greatgrandfather chatting to his neighbors in southern Italian dialect, a sociable man who did not learn English and who had no neighbors, or not ones anyone else could see. He was always poor and raised a son who was poor. The family stayed poor until my father came along, an accountant, a practical man who would never think to build a rowhouse in the middle of a field.

My five years in the Northwest are up and, predictably, I've grown to hate my job. I know I'd be a better and saner person if I lived where it didn't rain so much. I'm sick of the whole idea of salmon, the romanticization of a dumb fish leading what must be the world's most unexamined life. Anyway, the sky is gray and the salmon are mostly dead. I'm tired of it all. Though I've also run out of continent. Maybe I need to find a different way to run away.

My Cassill grandmother, the siren, told me it was always better to live in your head. She called it "metaphysics." She told me, with your mind you can control everything.

My grandmother felt pretty smug about controlling the world. She was not like my greatgrandfather, manipulating her environment and shaping the present into the mythic past (isn't the past always mythic?)

over and over again. She *was* like him in that she dealt with the present by paying no attention to it. I guess that's why she felt so good about things, though she didn't like her husband much and seemed only vaguely attached to her children. She loved her son Eddie and her grandsons but her fiercest and most absolute love was for moving around. She traveled constantly, alone, though she and my grandfather didn't have much money. She took cargo ships across the ocean; she stayed in redlight district hotels and listened to whores do business through the walls; she smoked opium and wore trousers. At seventy-nine she heard a niece had moved to Africa and took off for weeks, sleeping in a treehouse in Kenya. She never once brought back pictures.

My mother has never been adventurous like her mother, something my grandmother always humiliated her for. She's a timid woman. When I was growing up my mother would say of almost everything, "Don't say that." Pregnant, stupid, sick, crazy, little, big, dead, alive. She waged war against adjectives. Her mother had left her an awful burden. Thought made thing; utterance was an ongoing unbridled making. We walked together—we always walked, my mother didn't drive—with my mother trying to prevent me from changing anyone with my words.

I think my mother found it hard to reconcile the fact that she had made the world with the fact that she didn't like it very much. My grandmother made the world before the two world wars so maybe she felt good about that, that wars were the product of someone else's silly desires. Her world was clean. My mother's and mine was a mess of A-bombs and H-bombs and so many mosquitoes you fought them from daredevil aircraft, like they were this close to world conquest.

In fact, our world, or our country, kept declaring war. Against creeping communism, poverty, insects (malarial men coming back from the South Pacific dreaming of DDT), germs. Stains on clothes. War became our metaphor, only it wasn't because, except for the battle against poverty maybe, none of this metaphorical warfare we declared stayed metaphorical.

People fought with violence: airplanes, sprays, chemicals. They recruited with zeal. One of the recruitments was the Baby Boom, which my brother and my cousins and I belonged to, the plume of babies that followed the soldiers back from the second world war as if we'd been flushed from their wounds. American men had gone overseas and lost limbs and seen themselves die and come back filled with a desire to make new humans. For each of us boom children a soldier lay dead on a battlefield on another continent, and we corrected with our fat and harmless flesh what had been done to their bodies. We are all substitutions.

We played with GI Joe dolls, muscular sexless men in camouflage gear. Chris and Mark wore the crewcuts that made just about every boy our age look like a little Marine. When we outgrew dolls we played Risk, the board game of world conquest. I remember all of us hanging on the nightly news, waiting for the event that would trigger World War III. ("All it takes is China and Russia moving into Vietnam," Mark would say, leaning on the radio.)

Like many women my mother stuck out the war living at home with her parents, working, waiting for the return of her fiance—the Italian-American Catholic fiance from a poor family that her parents disapproved of. He planned to be an accountant, the first professional in a long line of peasants. My mother had a diamond and got letters and worked as a bookkeeper, waiting to be married. I picture her then, in that state of waiting for a new life that hasn't quite happened, when the things you do already half-hover in a mythical past. In love, I don't doubt. Miserable at home, I'm sure.

My mother lived through the war half in the future, at a remove from the life she was living and from that new life too. Several removes, it turned out. Her Italian-American Catholic fiance from a poor family—that her parents disapproved of—died overseas. Then she found another one and he became my father.

She heard the news about her fiance, Angelo, like this. My grandmother got the telegram and kept her mouth shut. They had a family supper, my mother and her parents and her sister Mildred. Then my mother washed the dishes while my grandmother dried them and as my mother washed, my grandmother told her bluntly that Angelo was dead. My mother paused a little and finished the dishes. She didn't say anything or cry and as usual she got the dishes clean. My grandmother told me this story when I was about fifteen.

"I find your mother terribly cold," she said reflectively, then added, "I never really knew your mother."

My mother's fiance had been shot in France during the invasion of Normandy. My father sailed in relative peace into Tokyo and helped occupy Japan. He didn't face real danger but I think the country itself breathed death and exhaustion and it filled him with a desire to make people. He met my mother after going to college on the GI bill. Above all he wanted to start a family.

Even among Italians my dad is a darkskinned man, the dark olive of the Middle East with exaggeratedly Italian features and blueblack curly hair he parts in the middle and oils into double waves. My mom is small, fineboned and fair, a tiny woman with a gruff voice and an air of muffled brooding pissed unhappiness about her. She tends to be an advocate of harsh and punitive things: capital punishment, sending political refugees back, ending welfare. It's a family trait. Her brother's always laying plans for lining up and shooting homeless people. My mother feels life hasn't treated her well, which seems odd in someone whose life was so carefully chosen, not once but twice.

What was to have been, she made again. Then watched the time she recaptured pass on, still out of her hands.

Under the rules of fiction I could recreate the dishwashing scene, the death of my mother's almost-husband. Under the rules of nonfiction I say, I imagine. Either way I'm not there, in the moment that begins my life.

Mary I'm sorry to tell you (soap clusters like seed on her wrist—no) I have to tell you—

There's something I dread having to tell you dear—(now that sounds like her)

There would be a plate, a piece of white ironstone suspended in the air, lambfat, seeds of Dawn or Ivory sliding into the sink. My grandmother checks my mother's reflection in the slick. Nothing.

My grandmother, as I said, got up early every morning at our shore cottage for a nude swim, until a few cottages rose up down the street. My mother has never been willing to undress even in front of my father. It's too easy to call them opposites: neither of them ever felt comfortable being female. My mother hid the awful fact and my grandmother thought her way out of it, traveling alone and unnoticed and inserting her body genderless into the male landscape. At home she was a woman. Away she was a figure in sensible shoes.

My grandmother treated two of her three daughters coldly, the other one just a bit better, and adored her son and grandsons. They could make a dent in the world, she said. She always believed in the power of men to effect change, sweetly agitate the stuff of the universe. Women could be cooks, she used to say, but only men could be chefs. Somehow she had a faith that by identifying so wholly with men she'd escaped being a woman herself. She discussed women in the third person as if, by taking her ego out of her body, that body lost its power to implicate her.

My mother too adores her son. My mother tells me that women are genetically barred from genius but can pass the genius gene to their sons. Women are genii of conception, their creation the work of the womb. Freudian—the son as vicarious penis—but I like to think of it as Shakespearean, women a bunch of Banquos getting kings though being none.

When my brother went away to college my mother moved into his room, twenty years later still half his things, half her things. She surrounds herself with scraps of his geology career, articles and research, typed his papers all through college, grabs his dirty clothes to wash—stuff men think women want to do but really women do when they realize the male country they've created is walled. So they smuggle things in, trivial things maybe but things they've touched. My mother's one trip is to pass this way.

I say "they" of these women because I've barred myself from being one of them. I just keep moving.

Ironically, my mother's family produces mostly women, at a fixed ratio of three to one, as if our organs were slot machines paying bets off at a bad rate. My mother has two sisters and one brother, and in my generation we're six girls and two boys. My mother deals with that by ignoring the girls until they get married, and then translating them into the lives of their husbands.

"How's Diana?" I say and she answers, "Ray's job is going well but he's gaining weight."

Now my parents take things that are true of me and associate them with Bruce: my passion for Shakespeare, whom Bruce doesn't care for, the famous writer I studied with, whom they brag Bruce studied with.

For Christmas they buy Bruce enormous books about Shakespeare.

"We know how much you love this," my mother says.

When we send probes into space to contact life elsewhere we include a male nude and a female nude. Leonardolike, with arms and legs splayed and their sex laid out, a few quick lines at the base of the torso. I wonder if anything seeing them could guess the story of these forms, the male that wants to bury in the female body this little limb that seems so ridiculously exposed, the female that wants to bury in the male body her spirit, that must feel so ridiculously exposed.

"Your brother's like me," my mother tells me, though of course he isn't. He'd never take another life as a substitute for his own.

All my adult life I've had the same nightmare. It comes back once a week at least, the kind of nightmare with a mood that sticks after you wake up. It's a nightmare where I'm a woman in advanced adulthood—thirties?—and still living with my parents. I'm miserable, stifled, desperate about being there and desperate to get away. Sometimes it ends on this note—I'm washing dishes or trudging up the stairs to my room—and sometimes I meet someone I half-like and think this is good enough, I can get out of here. I'll marry this person.

This dream's always confused me because I left home at nineteen and never went back, and married at twenty-five and knew years before I actually married who I would marry. I married the man I loved; in dreaming I face a chronic return of fears I've never had. Only now do I understand that I'm having my mother's nightmare. She never showed much feeling for my father. But nothing could have frightened her more than the prospect of a lifetime in her mother's house. She and my father met and married within a year. She was thirty-three.

Once you know where the dream comes from—the ten years or so my withdrawn mother spent in her parents' house between the death of Angelo and the arrival of my father—it seems obvious, heavy-handed. Less than deeply psychological I mean, just the reiteration of a feeling, boredom, being soaked in time. Washing dishes. Days without outside contact. A dull hope that for no reason at all something will happen. Panic inside.

The only secret to be unlocked is why this dream should have jumped into my head. It bears my mother's stamp. She hates symbols and even in dreams wouldn't, in her words, "hold with them": tolerate them. My own dreams are colorful, often violent, always bizarre. My mother married and had my brother within a year and me within three. Close enough to her days in the Cassill house, my grandmother's putdowns, the grinding fear. She'd have dreamed this dream a lot and it got into her blood and the blood flowed into her womb where I slept too. When I realized this fact I wondered how much else of her was in me, not the what-she-said-to-me and what-I-said-to-her stuff a shrink can pry out but what comes in through the blood and the cells. I think if I went through this story carefully enough I would find her writing through me, her own story.

Does this sound like a feminist fable? It's real and it frightens me. I thought I could be alone here, in the page's Quaker room. If my mother's dreams have been put into my head then all her narratives are there, and my grandmother's, and God knows who else's in my family: maybe more than my family. The suppressed, female presence of the reader, another one who lives through the story without a voice.

My mother has always kept the silence of Yahweh's name around Angelo. She's nearly eighty. I only learned his name last week. I knew vaguely of an old boyfriend but didn't know it had been an engagement or that he was dead till my teens. I did know from my parents' arguments that she kept Angelo's ring in a hidden drawer or compartment of her jewelry box. Recently with my mother full of wine we talked about it a little, oddly enough in Italy, where I went to teach temporarily, deferring my problem of the next move.

"How strange that you could have married him," I said tentatively.

"You would have been different," my mother said and grinned. I reminded her I would not have been at all.

"True," she said.

I'm sure it's these narratives that stay wrapped in a palpable silence that become something else. I don't speak in metaphor. I mean I think what the mouth doesn't void for the mind moves into the bloodstream and the nucleotides. It runs for the DNA as the only other form of language.

I've begun the painful, but I think necessary, process of examining my other dreams. Sometimes I have nightmares of having killed someone. I'm stuck with a heavy sticky corpse. I don't know what to do with it. Police come to the door. The corpse, gross and irreducible as a bloody sofa, won't leave my hands. Sometimes I dream of having children, a big irritating family, though I'm sterile. Whose lives are these? I don't know. It's clear now that whatever my ancestors have done and haven't told will continue to follow me, speaking in that gagged voice of things-that-return. And the last will be first, the quiet ones will be the loudest.

When my grandmother developed senile dementia she saw phantoms creep in through her windows and writhe around in her bed. If we visited, before we put her to sleep, we had to check the room for her, though of course in an hour or so she'd wake up screaming. She lived on cold toast and tea with evaporated milk, which she forgot and then drank hours later with the milk scummed into little islands. When I came I always found her with her hair stuck straight up and crumbs around her mouth and strange outfits on, a nightgown twisted over slacks. She still talked about her favorites constantly—dear dear Mark, dear dear Eddie—but couldn't seem to remember why she liked them so she just repeated her formula, "dear dear dear dear."

My mother is old now and has arthritis. I hold her arm and help her walk. It's the only time in my life I've been allowed to touch her, other than a peck at bedtime. I help her up stairs and down stairs and cook for her when I'm at her house. She knows my kindness is undeserved and sometimes it makes her nicer and sometimes not. Whatever her response I am steadily good. This is my form of the family cruelty.

I visited my senile grandmother often though I lived in upstate New York, Brooklyn, Atlanta. She remembered my husband well but not me really. That was fine. I'd become addicted to moving around, to people who didn't know me. I had my own perfect moment I kept repeating—moving, walking into a room that would be mine but wasn't yet, new apartments, new houses, admiring the pale empty walls. It's that moment, like with paper, when it shivers between receiving you and holds out the signs—the emptiness, the receptiveness and resistance—of another life, another story.

What was to have been she made again

Of course like all loves this one is based on illusion, the illusion of quiet, of nothing-there. Though once we exist nothing's empty; we can add but we can't subtract.

———

Here's Jim Morrison snarling, Waiting for the sunnnnn . . . .

"We'll hear it coming and we'll go down there, and it's just like a little tunnel, all bricks, and we'll stay and we'll never know when to get out," says Helen.

Mark says, "What do you want to bring with you?"

Chapter Five

Elizabeth

When the Toms River cancer cluster first made news—dying children in the headlines—it started a panic. People moved away, and houses for sale stayed for sale. Everyone drank bottled water. Local politicians got sick of the turmoil, of the story. A city councilman said, "No one is going to tell me we have more of a cancer rate than they do in Newark or Elizabeth."

Elizabeth, my other home and the first place I remember besides Holly Park, had a Queen's name. Every land's an extension of the monarch's body, a great green *I Am* of the royal person, and Elizabeth's city showed she'd been gone a long time. It was gassy and bad-smelling as any dead woman. Her skin—grass, buttercups, sweet-gums—had long ago been lost, closed over by a concrete embalming, which like any embalming didn't hold off decay but substituted one, more acceptable, kind of decay for another. It seemed prophetic that they went to the long-gone Renaissance to name this, a city that quickly became a great ungreen *I Am Not*. And I'm sure it galls that a place like Ocean County could compare to such a city and be found wanting.

Our neighborhood in Elizabeth was called Elmora. Our street, Lower Road, was a block of rowhouses broken into apartments. We had a first floor two-bedroom—one bedroom for my parents, one for my brother and me—with a small dining area/parlor that looked out onto the street. A huge Evergreen Cemetery bulked at us across Lower Road—a weedy urban cemetery, without the precise sentiment of the suburbs but only plastic flowers in pickle jars and a huge vague melancholy in the epitaphs. So loved, they said. So special. So missed.

The Evergreen seemed in permanent dialogue with the young mothers sitting on their stoops on my side of the road, painting their nails arterial red, pinning rollers in their hair and shushing babies. A sign at the Evergreen gate that faced us inexplicably warned *No Food* and *Absolutely No Cooking*.

It's a contamination to eat with the dead, like you're trying to share with them something they can't share, or shouldn't.

Elizabeth has an air like no other air—heavy, gray, like an odor become a scarf wrapped around your face: an olfactory purdah.

The city, and Newark, which squats next to it, survives on heavy industry. They're amazing cities to see from far away: the rows of long smokestacks sticking up like goosenecks, breathing black clouds that roll together to become a lower level of the atmosphere. Sluices dripping muddy brown sludge matter-of-factly into the water. I remember how many days, especially in the summer, began with the radio declaring our air quality unacceptable. Like you had a choice about whether or not to breathe.

Most of the plants are oil refineries and paint factories. I have vivid memories of crossing the bridge to New York, watching the Little Dutch Boy smile mindlessly as fumes turned slow somersaults around his painted form. I try to identify the smell of the place: sulfur, something mustardy, something corrosive. In its heaviness, its moist almost oily presence, it reminds me of the ashes of my Italian grandfather's fourth wife. We cremated her and tried to sprinkle her ashes on the sea when a wind blew up. My grandfather had too many wives for me to get sentimental about them, but I remember the utter surprise when she blew back in our faces, mine and my family's: an ash fine as confectioner's sugar, black, greasy in its cling. We inhaled her, brushed her off our lips.

"Oh," my mother said, "Marcie," as if Marcie had formed out of the little cyclone of her dust. Maybe in Elizabeth we inhaled the body of a dead queen.

Wondering what to do with the can of ash that had been Marcie brought her closer to me than she'd ever been in life. The can—a cardboard tube—sat on my parents' mantel for a year before we could figure out what to do with it. It came packed in a stiff brown carton and arrived from the mortician's a few months before my wedding, so Bruce and I flayed it open, thinking it was a gift. Bruce held up the tube, a sticker on it printed with the word *CONTENTS:*, where someone had carefully written out Marcelle Antonetta. We put her on the mantelpiece.

I didn't have much contact with my father's father, who had lost my father's mother to a damaged heart and his next two wives to cancer. He moved away from New York when I was seven, to a doublewide in

Vero Beach, Florida. We once drove down there. His house smelled bad because he had hundreds of parakeets in cages stacked one on top of the other, plus it was loud because the parakeets never shut up. People could drive on the beach, and all day pickups pulled up to the water with paper bags of their garbage and dumped it. I was ten or eleven and hated the place. Marcie (I don't remember the other wives) always quoted supermarket tabloid stories, telling me one day that cats really had nine lives, and showing me the article. She got on my nerves, an adult and dumber than I was, dumber even than my little cousins.

My grandfather and Marcie moved back up north when I was in my twenties. In between we had very little contact with him though my father sent him money. I know my grandfather had a twenty-year feud with his youngest son, my uncle Larry, and never saw or spoke to him, and that he died without reconciling. We didn't see or speak of Larry either, I guess as a consequence. Other than my aunt Phil and her brood we didn't see much of my father's family, though they were all close by. My father blamed that on his mother's early death. She died when he was in his twenties, of a rheumatic heart. He said no family could stay together without a good woman at its head.

Elizabeth's cemetery, a vacant lot and eventually Robert Morris Grammar School defined my life, and my brother's. We raced to school past the factions of kids waiting to beat up other factions of kids. We bought candy at Gould's on the corner. Each phone pole flapped with staplegunned flyers. The one I remember best showed a middle-aged man, a WASPy face, bland, cleanshaven, with the words *This man is a childkiller* under him.

Our everyday playground was the vacant lot, just a little larger than a driveway, weedy and full of broken glass. A speck of a cell of the larger body, but we loved it. We brought Legos and dolls and played there every day. But my brother, Chris, and I loved the cemetery most. We weren't allowed to go there—drug dealers used it—but we snuck over pretty often anyway. "I'm goin down Gould's," Chris told my parents, then walked down Lower Road a little way, shuttling across the street to the Evergreen.

The cemetery seemed like the one thing that had been built with our needs in mind. Lots of concise, simple English; everything eye level; four and five foot tombs, carved with droopy angels, that looked like luxury cottages built to our scale. On the Lower Road side of the cemetery a huge grave of black marble—three-pillared, kind of a triptych—dwarfed the others; it had brass musical notes and LPs stuck all over it. *Singin' Sam,* read the plaque, *Singer, Songwriter, Peacemaker.* A muse was loose somewhere.

I felt an odd allegiance to Elizabeth the queen. I liked to read about her. She had herself played the muse for male courtiers, through an act of will much like the one that produced such a grave in a city with little use for songwriting, peacemaking, or singin'. Ralegh praised Elizabeth's "snowe and silke" beauty, though a German visitor wrote of her indifferent features and black, utterly black, teeth. Courtiers called her the Sun Queen.

I've written poems to my Elizabeth, Elizabeth the place. My father'll say to me, "Can't you take out Elizabeth and put in Fanwood?" Fanwood is the suburby suburb where my parents live now, in a splitlevel painted loud colors inside, with various shag carpetings: orange, brown and yellow twists in the living room, watercolors crowded on the walls.

I say No because I never lived there. They moved in during my second year away at college.

"But we live in Fanwood," my father says, continuous present.

Here is the harmony between my father's and my mother's families: rearranging. My cousin Helen, my mother's murdered aunt, her uncle Frederick, and my father's brother Larry all gone. Them, along with countless cousins and aunts and uncles who appear and disappear and whom I lose track of, hauled in and out of our own private Tower of London. When I say we don't speak of them I mean literally, don't speak. I'm sure my parents have their versions of them, though, ghosts of their ghosts, or faces or voices or steps that reappear at odd hours. My revenant is a city.

Elizabeth was my grammar school home, my aboriginal home, my prepuberty home. Partway through my childhood my father bought a house in a bluecollar suburb at the edge of the city. We moved, and soon I got to middle school. My sphere of action shifted irrevocably to my own body. It produced brackish blood each month, it grew conical and fat on top, it felt alive below when I thought about other bodies. I had something called a *bust* where a chest had been, *pubes* where my legs met. I had a menses and pelvic exams where my friendly doctor began vising me apart. I felt overhauled, like a car being remodeled, parts ripped out and replaced with new parts, fattier, touchier and the objects of obsessed attention from those around me. My friend Lisa's mom stood by her at every pelvic exam, right up at her labia, to make sure, Lisa said proudly, she didn't get "broken."

This looking, this weird scrutiny and obsessed protection, tamponaded me inside myself: there was no way out. I spent time thinking about my own face. I thought about my body, which had suddenly contracted, become painful and specific and, at the same time, weaker. In Elizabeth Elizabeth itself had been my body, or seemed like it, physically, as it had been the queen's metaphorically: my sphere of action, my center. I treated it carelessly, as one big sharded extension of myself. I left my stuffed animals in the lot, and Barbie dolls and Barbie clothes on gravestones.

Childhood is external, adolescence and adulthood are internal. In Elizabeth smokestacks poured up thick plumes, men killed children, Singin' Sam stayed strangely quiet. I took it all in, the way I accepted my hands lifting Babe Ruths to my face. How to argue? It was all there, laid out like anatomy. It seemed to be both outside me and within my head.

The cemetery gave Chris and me a psychic as well as a physical focus. It was in a sense two cemeteries, and we kept them separate—the cemetery aboveground and the one below. The first cemetery delighted us: a marble and cement playground with lots of trees and plastic flowers, and though we loved to play dead we never did around the graves. Not to avoid being ghoulish but because we found the place cheerful, a little childsized city waiting for its population to drift in. We never forgot the other cemetery, the resting ground of the dead my parents told us about, we just never thought about it when we were actually there. At bedtime, though, my normally sweet brother sent me off with stories of our neighbors, our departed who weren't so much departed as very close by, boxed and held with just a little frosting of dirt.

"They come out at night," he used to tell me, adding solemnly, "They'll eat you."

They wouldn't eat him, he said, because girls tasted better.

That cemetery marked me. I sleep with a sheet up over my face still, folded so a little channel of air can reach my nose—looking ridiculous, a Muslim woman entering the marketplace of dreams—as I learned to do then, in some belief that the scrap of sheet would protect me. Though I don't play in cemeteries now.

Chris and I don't talk the way we did, when "wouldn't eat him" would have come out *wudden eaddum*. We've moved on. We're professionals. We try to talk like newscasters: that accent that implies you didn't grow up anywhere, but sprang fullblown into the realm of the commercial. I love New Jersey accents, though saying so proves how far away I am.

So he says to me, he says, What? And I says to him, I says, What What!! I love the instinctive use of the present tense, the immediacy, the way dialogue is insisted on as dialogue.

My dad, who's retired, has been losing his job English and reverting to his father's English, the immigrant English of Brooklyn. It's kind of existential. Nothing gets *through* for my father anymore, it gets *true*. The New York Thruway has been exalted to the *Trueway*. His language reframes the world as a Pilgrim's Progress. Everything imperfect, even thin soup, is a *sin*. He calls me to talk about his garden.

"Everything's comin good," he says, adding, "The *mulenyans* is comin up good," using a dialect form of the Italian *melanzana*, "eggplant."

My cousin Anna Marie goes the other way. She gets a secretarial job and works to upgrade her speech.

"When we got to the place whereas we was goin," she begins a story. And she says all the time, "I says to myself I says, Self . . . "

I can't bring myself to lose *come by us*. It means come to us, come over: *come by us at six*, and I notice myself when I say it. It sounds so paradoxical, so deconstructionist, as if you request the opposite of what you request: for people to just miss you rather than visiting at all, to slow their cars perhaps, give you an instant of lingering attention, then go about their own business.

———————

Those posters didn't tell the whole truth about the childkiller. He didn't kill all children, just little girls. He didn't molest the girls or dally with them but murdered them quickly. He seemed to be a figure from one of my brother's nightly stories, an Evergreen ghoul, lingering in broad daylight and undissuaded by sheets. He was the word made flesh.

His first victim, a seven-year-old named Wendy Sue Wollen, was walking with her mother on a street in downtown Elizabeth when the mother moved a few feet off to look in a window. The childkiller must have kept a knife on him. He marched up to Wendy Sue, purposeful but not dramatic, and sank it into her stomach: then dissolved like the regular man he was, back into the regular crowd.

Wendy Sue Wollen never knew she'd been stabbed. No one else did either, not for a few minutes. She said, That man punched me, and repeated it a few times, bent over a little and bleeding out between her fingers, thinking some guy had just walked up to her and, for no good reason, socked her one. Then she collapsed and died.

I was also seven. Soon the man stabbed another little girl on a playground. Our lives went on Childkiller Alert. My father instructed my mother to walk us kids to and from school, though after a week or so she grew plainly annoyed about it. The childkiller was never caught; the cops finally gave up and announced he must have moved on, to another city. My mother, always the pragmatist, had long since quit the escort business. To me, the man never left but joined the physical world of Elizabeth, my extended self. A jowly man, not angry looking but uncle-y, benign in that semi-abstracted adult way, like he could be selling insurance or Fuller brushes or handing you licorice. Like a wound could be just another inscrutable adult gift. When men passed me on the street my abdomen grew tender.

———

Kikes, krauts, Polacks, wops, hunks, greaseballs. In my neighborhood we had ricks, spicks, micks, nips, jigs, chinks, ricans, hicans. And of course niggers and the much more common mooleys, another corruption of *melanzana*. Negotiating ethnic names was a precise skill and one we picked up early. We kids all used them, often of ourselves, and other than the really loaded *kike* and *nigger* none were off limits. A mixture of tone and body language signaled whether a word was meant to be aggressive. Most of the time it wasn't, just descriptive, and would be taken that way. "You a kraut?" "You a rican?" were ordinary conversation. Add "ugly" or somesuch to it, and lots of emphasis and a friendly look—"You ugly mick!"—and the use became affectionate. When I was a kid and I first met my friend Alice's mother, she said, "Oh, you've really got that guinea nose."

I had a Greek aunt, a Puerto Rican aunt, an Irish uncle, a West Indian grandfather, Jewish cousins; I could usually find some connection to people. Down the shore my aunts and uncles sat around needling each other.

What's a seven-course meal to an Irishman? *(A six-pack and a baked potato)*

How did Mussolini get eight bullets in him? *(Seventy-five Italian sharpshooters)*

When Jackie K. married Ari Onassis my aunt said darkly, "It won't last. She doesn't know the Greeks."

Our part of Ocean County had a lot of immigrants and children of immigrants, especially Italians and Poles. An old Italian couple bought the lot next door to ours and set up a bait and candy shop, with a couple of pool tables and pinball and ice cream. Fat Mrs. Schipano bent over to dip out the cones, sweat rolling down from her forehead into the chocolate and strawberry and vanilla.

Ethnicity in all its forms was part of our talk, holding the place jobs hold in other American cultures, or your therapist and your feelings, or what part of town you're in. "What are you?" was a standard conversation starter, our version of "What do you do?" We loved—love— declarative sentences about the self. Even a question about how you eat an Oreo might spin off an "I am" answer.

"I'm not the kind of person who likes cubbyholes," my dad says about a desk, and, I'm not a person who stays up late. I'm a people person. I'm not a sit-arounder, I'm a doer.

When people asked me about my background I'd say, "Well, my mother's mother was English and her father was from Barbados and she met my father, who's Italian." All that distance plummeting somehow into my body. Though the person I talked to always knew someone who came from a village near some branch of my family's village, or at least pretended to know someone.

We reached for connections, we worked them out, even where they barely existed, because so many of us had a dizzying sense that there was no one else like us, not really. My grandfather was a British subject of a colonized Caribbean island who'd also been Canadian and American; his wife was an English Christian Scientist. My father's grandfather came here from a remote village and stayed to set up his shadow family, his rhyme children, in Brooklyn. His son my grandfather had a fourth-grade education and worked as a gravedigger and mechanic, or driving truckloads of dynamite for minimum wage, when he could find work.

I played with a girl named Renee, whose parents had both been held in concentration camps in Germany. My friend Barb's Armenian grandparents fled the Turkish massacre. We talked all the time about our families, each with her own portion of family bitterness.

"Your hair is like mine," Renee said to me once.

Renee had wiry, black hair, nothing like mine. Our resemblances were fleeting and coincidental. So we accepted these metonyms of what we were—greaseballs, dagos, yids—and carried on from there.

Elizabeth was realms within realms. The lot, the cemetery, home, other places. We often went to Peterstown, the Italian section a few miles away. Once a year, in August, Peterstown erupted in a nine-day street fair honoring St. Rocco, the city's patron. Rocco appeared on posters for the feast: a sad-looking fellow lifting up his robe to show what looked like a skinned knee. The Virgin Mary seemed like more of a go-getter, paraded through the streets with her gilt crown, streamers of dollar bills covering her plaster body, along with rhinestone jewelry glittering in its colorless way, armloads of Timexes: all gifts of the faithful. Like a new incarnation of the spirit, beyond flesh and into cash. Such abundance marked St. Rocco's. Rides; music; vendors selling sandwiches of sweet and hot sausages roasted with onions and peppers, the sausage blackened and the onions and peppers caramelized in olive oil; deepfried *zeppole* dredged in sugar. Sometimes the packed crowd would bend like the muscle of a snake, and in the middle you'd see a knot of old women, short and plump, bouncing like black balloons as they danced the tarantella.

In warm weather we went to Peterstown for the Sneaker Lady, an old Italian lady in tennis shoes who mixed up lemon and orange ice in a huge wooden churn. She stood in front of an ancient storefront, a five-and-dime or something, selling ices, which tasted like fruit wearing its glorious heavenly form: itself but intense, cool in the asphalt heat, perfectly sweetened. We went to other Italian neighborhoods: Newark, Little Italy in Manhattan. My father liked Poppalardo's in Little Italy for bread. Poppalardo's sold round loaves with crust an inch thick knobbing up all over it. The bakery also had Italian loaves six feet long, smudged with cornmeal and alive with sesame seed. Once we brought one to my aunt Philomena's house, and my father and brother carried it in across their shoulders, like pioneers.

After we moved to Roselle Park I didn't have much contact with Elizabeth, until I hit fourteen and fifteen and started going there to drink.

Roselle Park bars were pretty relaxed about the drinking age, but Elizabeth bars were even more relaxed, as well as cooler and scarier, and if they hassled you you could zip across the Goethals Bridge to Staten Island, where the drinking age was eighteen and nobody ever got carded. We liked a bar called the Hearth, pronounced the Heart', on Westfield Avenue. Bikers hung out there, and greasers, and junkies, who liked their drinks sweet as Kool-Aid. If I went with all girls we'd have drinks in front of us practically as soon as we walked through the door.

"He likes you," my friend Bonnie would say, of whomever: "He thinks you're a little Lo-Lee-Ta."

None of us knew who Lo-Lee-Ta was.

Girls drank sloe gin fizzes or 7&7s; guys, junkies excepted, drank beer or whiskey, or beer and whiskey together in boilermakers, or tequila. Often we'd go from Elizabeth bars to Staten Island bars, weaving across the Goethals Bridge on the backs of motorcycles. Smokestacks rose around us spewing out their fumes, that heaviest substance that could go by the name of air.

When I quit going to high school I spent even more time at the Heart, which I forgot was really called the Hearth. I couldn't have spelled anything then. The word Elizabeth itself came out Elizabet', slur on the e, so it sounded, not inaccurately, a lot like Loseabet.

A few years ago my husband and I were heading through Elizabeth to Manhattan. On a side street a guy drove into us, very matter-of-

factly, as if we'd asked him to. We got out; he got out. He had the clas-
sic Loseabet look: boiled. Eyes at half mast. He had no insurance, so
we decided to clear out.

"I'm sorry man," he said like an echolalic: "Gimme your number
I'll give it to ya next check. I'm sorry man sorry man sorry man sorry
man hey, sorry, man."

I'm 40 now. Everyone I know is going back somewhere, digging for
roots, sifting through old soil. Though I think about Holly Park and
dream about it and go there, I only went back once to Elizabeth, driving to Elmora to visit my neighborhood. Nothing had changed: the
cemetery, the apartments, even the weedy scabby lot. That sameness
sounds comforting but wasn't. I stood looking at the place—the glass
glitter and old brick and *No Cooking* sign—waiting for it to tell me if I
had loved it or hated it. It looked back, not seeming to care much one
way or another.

> I disagree with Eliot. The end of the journey is returning to the starting
> point and not knowing it for the second time. Letting that seep in.
> Absorbing its silence. Evergreen Cemetery: Plastic & scratchy dacron
> flowers. Drooping Marys & rhyming couplets ("Weep not for me/I wait
> for thee"). Singin' Sam's triptych monument covered with jaunty brass
> musical notes, a stone record with birth & death dates, flushed 8" x 10"
> photo, "Singer, Songwriter, Peace Maker," a carved stone & brass electric
> guitar. Death the saccharine mother, the unflagging dance partner.
> (6/30/87, age 30)

Once in a while I still eat in Peterstown. It's also the same. Elizabeth's a low-income city, with no tax base for the kind of strip
mall/office park development that would edit me out of its landscape.
The city waits like a childhood room preserved by a mother crazy with
nostalgia. It forces me to individuate, to cut myself free.

Of course, to do that I have to define somewhere else as my place, stop, scatter the pepper off my feet.

"You're Spanish," a woman said to me last night.

People guess Mexican, Greek, Latina, Italian, other things, like Finnish and Russian. A man once got belligerent when I told him I wasn't Jewish. "You are," he said, "obviously."

"Exotic," my husband says. More to the point, children have pointed to me and said, *witch*. Once, when I gave a lecture at another school, a strange blank woman came up to me and told me my evil thoughts had no power there.

I wonder, if I had uttered some curse, if she'd be suffering with it, feeling a graveyard fly at her through the air: or expecting to die at the hands of an ordinary man in broad daylight, or calling herself a queen, a Renaissance queen. I believe I have swallowed these things, and they erupt in my face: dark heavylidded eyes, hooked nose, bow lips, pale skin, each dying to tell its story. My mother's West Indian family defined itself by its hatred of Catholics, then she went ahead and married one, producing two children who grew and grew, oversized, much bigger than either parent: as if all our cells could figure out was division.

I remember faces well and honestly, my own and others': Queen Elizabeth's staunch, serene, whippetnosed, lips clamped around her teeth. The pouchy placid face of the childkiller, and the Virgin Mary's otherworldly face, floating above her dress of money. I remember eating graveyard dirt when I was a child, and inhaling my grandfather's fourth wife, and inhaling the city. We drank and ate the sediment of photos from the Denzer & Schafer plant, drank and ate the image. What does my body consist of?

I bet myself I'd never miss the place. But even my computer stores the word as *Elizabet.* Loseabet.

It's much safer where I live now. Children don't have to worry walking to school. I see them streaming off each morning, a parade of fair heads, mainly of Dutch or German descent, each no doubt with his or her own mouthful of sorrow. I miss mine. I miss the mingling. A place where everyone frictioned together in a small space, not just people of different races and ethnic groups but even the dead and the hopelessly evil, the ones so evil they lost a sense of themselves, and dressed as if evil itself were a job.

My friend Maureen and I compare our childhoods. She's vibrant and pretty with a face that fits together, and she's from Kalispell, Montana.

"I miss it," she says of Montana. "The landscape's compelling. Open space and rivers."

When I ask her about returning she says, "It's the culture . . . the racism. I can't go back."

I can't go back either, though I'm much less sure of what compels and repels me.

There's not much I'd call landscape in my part of New Jersey. Even the rivers hardly feel like rivers, running along banks of factories like big sluiceways for industrial waste. We have racism but not exactly Maureen's us-them racism: our stereotypes often come self-generated, Jews telling you they're cheap, Poles they're dumb. Partly they're internalizing the larger culture, partly grasping that an edge is near—sensing the vertiginous drop out of something, anything, and into nothing at all.

I imagine the childkiller thinking that in one swift instant he'd established himself, become a word.

Chapter Six

Springs

Elizabeth's a port city, a city that grew up around a harbor. There's still an Elizabethport, though visitors following the signs wouldn't find much that's natural about it. The Hudson River's been so claimed it's another runny artery for the industry of New York and New Jersey. But it matters, as water, a starting point.

To talk about how we live you have to talk about water, that it's two-thirds of our bodies and of the earth and very devious stuff. It waits to bolt down from the sky and break you, and tinder you or your ship. In the body your H_2O waits to accept tritium, a radioactive isotope of hydrogen, to become unstable tritiated water, leaving lesions in your cells. It's a human weakness to love water, though among earthly things it's the cur waiting to bite the hand.

Talk about the word, *water,* how it's *war* and *'twer* and *wear.*

When I was very young I saw a boy drown on Holly Park Beach. No, that's wrong, he lived. But I swear the child who woke up couldn't have been the same. The boy, who had dark hair, seven years and a bit of pudge on him, was swimming and then wasn't—humped and floating facedown in the water. Some teenager dragged him out and did mouth-to-mouth. The drowning boy had slateblue skin and slate, swollen lips; wherever you'd expect to see the rose of his blood the ink of Barnegat Bay had dyed him.

My father fulminated for days after that, about the boy's mother. She'd been preoccupied, turning her fingernails into pink planets with stuck white moons. He said it was her fault.

In Italy I saw a boat, like a trawler, with a dredge attached and the dredge was pulling something long and black and limp from the water: a dead man in a diving suit. He had been diving to see an underwater statue of Jesus (tall and skinny, with upstretched arms) when he died, and his name was Pellegrino, which means Pilgrim.

This happened in the tiny fishing village of San Fruttuoso in Liguria, a place you reach by ferry. The name means Saint Fruitful. It's tiny but peelingly pretty and many people go to dive to the statue, Jesus of the Depths—a bronze considered the protector of divers. This Jesus stands underwater like he's playing catch; the pedestal sinks in the muck and the arms rise. He's like something caught between gravity and sheer will. Around him the weird still psalming of anemones that open and close their mouths. I don't remember his face at all. We saw pictures.

When the dredge pulled its find from the water I said, "I think it's a man."

Chris said, like a brother, "Don't be stupid."

Bruce said, "A tire."

We found the story—and the name—in a newspaper the next day.

Lorenzo Pellegrino died like a man in a trashy novel: the pilgrim, the weeds, the Jesus. I felt sorry for him, though I guess dying people don't have time to reflect on the irony of their death. Unless all that stuff about time slowing down is true. I hope it isn't because it wouldn't be comforting, to watch your edges dissolve into anecdote, the most finite thing of all.

Likewise, because it's existence, conception has everything to do with water and nothing to do with love.

On Halloween of 1992 Bruce and I flew to Atlanta for a funeral. His grandfather had died. Bruce's parents had been dead for decades and he had no other family but a brother and sisters. His grandfather was nothing like mine, always far away with one fragile wife or another. Bruce's grandfather had been a loveable man, very present in Georgia where all the family lived but us, sweetly domineering, always forcing us to sit and eat Moon Pie after Moon Pie.

We got the news of his death on our answering machine and booked a flight, forgetting the date and season. At the United Airlines check-in the darksuited women wore skeleton pins. One had a skeleton t-shirt, the kind that would shine in the dark, under her suit, like the woman offered either sympathy or ridicule. They could not stop giggling.

What is your costume?

I go as a mourning man.

That's not what we said.

Stewards and stewardesses had bone pins too, and made ooo-oooing sounds as they sluiced out our coffee. The whole flight from the West Coast was like that: people around us refused to be anything but absurd. One stewardess had dark hair and lips pinked to a triangle, no mouthskin visible; when she leaned over me her earrings jangled, each a glad skeleton though she with her soft layers had no humor about her. Candy corn materialized on our tray tables. We felt not only the loss of a man but of our right context. We'd been stuck in the death days calendar.

My husband's twin, David, drove us to his house. I noticed something I've noticed every year since—out of the flow of kids skirting doublefile down the street for Halloween, the number of them dressed as serial killers. Not real ones but ones we've invented to amuse ourselves, the ones that butcher teenagers in movies: Jason with his hockey mask and buzzsaw, the fingernail guy Freddy, someone demonic whose head is pins.

David couldn't stop talking about Big Gay's death. It crept out with whatever he said, like a mouthful of smoke.

We heard a noise and he said, "There really is a death rattle. It's a buzz right *here.*

"He talked to other things in the room. He didn't even look at us," David said, narrowing his eyes in calculation. He's a reporter with the Atlanta paper, and seemed to wonder if he should have asked questions.

Inside my uterus, after years of trying to have this happen, a group of cells had begun to divide and divide. They'd been doing that for several months and at this point some would have called the group sentient, though it too couldn't be said to know irony. We did. We held these things together like they were images in a poem: the death date, the children dressed as the killers of children, the bones used as ornaments and in counterpoise, a speck alive inside. It was my third month, the time when you start to think of the thing floating around in there with purpose, feeling its way, like a diver. With a rope winding out of it, a lifeline out of that sea.

———

The poem we put together, or that our lives were putting together, was a bad poem, corny. Even at the time I knew that, and a distant part of me wanted to rearrange, to aestheticize. Get rid of Halloween and make it something more interesting, like Michaelmas. My life grated in my own ear.

My lower abdomen started hurting the next day, All Soul's. A biblical pain, like torches. I could hardly move and instead of the funeral went to the hospital.

I'll tell you what I'm not seeing Fluid is the element of irony, always restless, carving our earth and retracting, licking out cliffs and gorges, leaving us to climb the outline of its history. It's forced by its nature to congeal and evaporate into other things, and that's where irony begins, in that deeprooted irritation. There's nothing about the first fluid stage of life that's not literary: the bloodfeeding, the cord, the heart that begins its life outside the body and migrates in. What I see as a team of doctors ultrasounds my abdomen is the pearshaped space where the human body exists both entirely on the symbolic level and on its own terms—*I'm not seeing a heartbeat*

I went from the hospital to a clinic. When they hooked me up to an ultrasound again all the doctors and nurses and techs packed in to look. They spoke to one another (I'll tell you what I'm not seeing) but not to me.

The one doctor I recall has no face. I remember his hands. Plump, very white, almost gleaming, loaded with fat rings. They moved the transducer around on my stomach with economy, pointed and then nested against his white jacket in a kind of sympathetic communion. He never looked at my face. He delivered his medical assessment to Bruce and refused to speak to me. To be frank, I was crying, and at the time I forgave and respected his need to ignore me, a woman who could not control her fluid interior or her fluid exterior. He expected the pregnancy had aborted itself, he said, not seeing a heartbeat.

The doctor told Bruce, a twin, that the pregnancy had been multiple, triplets at least. Back home in Bellingham, where the miscarriage was confirmed and the remains surgically scraped out, my doctor said almost certainly quads. Naturally occurring, a one-in-half-a-million chance. Several doctors asked me—*I'll tell you I'm not*—if I secretly took fertility drugs.

We live in the expectation we'll keep living, that's all there is to it. That because of the mystery or freakery of genetics our existence is like water's, which keeps going in changed but familiar forms: snow, ice, aquifer, the patterns we call *frostflowers* on the window. *E unum pluribus.* We put the matter of our body out there like H_2O molecules pushing themselves to the surface of a lake, to be plucked off by the air and reshaped. It doesn't matter how different the difference is, it is us. Though some molecules keep fretting on the surface, untouched. What we're not seeing: a heartbeat of something beyond us and of us, locking itself to the landscape.

In the eighties and nineties the Cassill girls started trying to conceive. We started mindlessly, flowingly. Our mothers had poured out kids. Some, like me—born of a mad rush around plastic and jelly—poured out when they didn't want us. Only two of the six of us had children, one of the two with difficulty. Three, including me, went through fertility treatments. No matter: our seed rocked alone on its ocean. We had endometriosis, misformed organs. Long before they announced the cancer cluster, the autism cluster, the leukemias and breast cancers of Ocean County, we thought of water, or I did. Pitcher after pitcher of shorewater Tang, scented with rotted egg. Helen and I leaning in, pouring boiling water over the dinner dishes. My uncle Eddie bottling tapwater up and taking it home "for the iron." The crabs, the blowfish, the scavengers we pulled from the bay. Other places, like Love Canal, where the unborn went seepingly off. *I'll tell you what I'm not. I'm not.* Seeing this, finally.

My husband's grandfather was named Gay Leming, pronounced with a short "e," a name that tickled us. It's a myth, I know, that lemmings jump off cliffs—they're just swarmers whose quick departures the human eye reads as suicide—but it's a good addition to the myth, that they'd go gaily.

When Big Gay (called Big to separate him from Bruce's sister Gay) died, we had just moved to Bellingham, after a year of living in Ohio and Virginia in a dreamy frenzy of contracting our lives to fit in small brown boxes and expanding them to fill houses again. We lived in four houses in one year. Wherever we were, we drove to Atlanta to see Big Gay, who lived in a nursing home and had contracted to the point of his body and a few dingy photographs. We stayed for long visits, spending a few days each at the houses of Bruce's siblings, babysitting, doing chores like buying Big Gay his wheelchair.

We visited Big Gay twice a day in the home, a long low institutional building of beige brick, the unmistakable odors of hospital and urine. The residents spent the day wheeled together in a gigantic room, immobile, white hair flying over peeling skulls, some slumped forward, some staring or babbling.

One named Lulu shrieked, "Too late! Too late! Uh Oh Oh uh OH." If you got close to her she'd grab your hand and kiss it.

Like a museum of the degradation of the human body, I wrote in my diary.

It's awful to see Big Gay this way. Sunday we wheeled him outside, in front of a bed of red & white impatiens. It was very warm, & we brushed bees and flies away from our faces. I don't think I have much time left, Big Gay said, very evenly. I put a flower in his lapel.

He was feeble, 110 pounds and losing, unable to put himself on the toilet. Sometimes he said incoherent things like, "There's a riot in the basement!" and sometimes he returned to lucidity and talked about what he called the happiest time of his life, when he and his wife lived in Atlanta and Bruce and the others were kids.

I wonder how conscious he was of happiness then . . . it seems like something we fit into the past, into the spaces where no pain occurs.

That's what I thought at the time.

Big Gay said to us one day, "You know, you go along and you struggle, and then you look back and realize you weren't struggling at all, it couldn't have been more fun." Then he fell asleep.

One day I went from sitting with Big Gay to sitting with our newborn nephew Zachary, rocking him in a portable carseat you push with your foot, thinking about them both: helpless, in diapers, whimpering under tufts of hair. Loveable in the child, I wrote, repulsive in the adult.

Who wants to be reminded of our melting back into the womb, as if we never came out of it?

That was October 1991. A year later Big Gay died in the nursing home. For a few months he'd gone back to live in a studio apartment, then one day David stopped by and found him ready, snappish, with a tiny suitcase packed. "I've been waiting to go back in!" He said, I'm ready to die now, and did. He never knew we didn't have our baby.

At forty I can't stop thinking about when things happened or will happen, dates, instants. Like death dates, those days that sit innocently in the calendar with birthdays, subverting them. To know when things occurred, quietly, below the surface, that couldn't be undone. It's become essential (as well as impossible) to see the moment when my biological children were lost, when the eggs I was born with took on the role of bodily excreta.

In 1984 my family received a letter from the county telling us to quit drinking from our well. We brought bottled water down sometimes but mostly ignored the warning, having decided long ago that shore-water was therapeutic. And no one bothers with bottled water for things like tea, toothbrushing, showers, during which the average person can inhale or receive through the skin quarts of water. So we all kept ingesting the water and it becomes in the nineties my obsession to find out why our well was declared unsafe, as if that answer won't be just another set of questions. I worked as a journalist once. I have reporting skills. I make telephone calls, hour after hour of them. Mostly I listen to message machines. EPA sends me to DEP, which sends me to ATSDR, which sends me to the county Board of Health, which says it has no records. Finally I talk to a very pleasant man named Foreman.

"There was the lead in Berkeley wells, but that was earlier," he says. "All I can think is Denzer & Schafer—that's nearby, so it would make sense, but the official word is no wells were closed."

Didn't it contaminate the groundwater? Yes it did.

Of course my infertility could have happened in my mother's body, the DDT, the swimming in Toms River, by the chemical pipeline leading into the woods.

There are facts that float without anything beneath them and even if you could tie them to the rock of a real event, no one would know what that might mean. It would only leave pretty ripples, circles to follow.

———

The vague, unformulated, untheorized, unthought-out world
wrote a film critic. The difficulty of talking about what happens—
the births and deaths, the gestating, generating, poisoned bodies—is
its shapelessness, its obvious, surface movements. The mirror art holds
up to nature isn't reflection but containment. A means of edging.

I wrote a piece about the miscarriage and an editor sent it back,
calling it "raw." He suggested I lose the death or the multiple pregnancy, or both.

DDT, heroin, dioxins, quadruplets. The poem of this body is a bad
poem, trite.

The more I bore myself the more the world fascinates me, with its
comically bad taste. Nowhere is this more true than in Italy, where I
seem to end up a lot, working or just living. My life there becomes
wildly overstated, full of omens, Felliniesque. Nothing's subtle. The
museums and churches bear up with impressive state their cargo of
gory men and women, saints and Christs. St. Stephen stands calm, lips
parted, two rocks buried in his brain. St. Peter Martyr inclines his
head to listen, ears intact though his skull's been divided in two by a
cleaver that still juts out of it, framed by a dainty spray of blood.

On a train heading from Venice to Rome a Neapolitan couple boarded
my compartment while I slept, with their baby son. I woke up to a
sound—a "ss, ss" between the teeth—the father made to his boy, and I
woke up into the past because my Italian grandfather used to make
that sound to me when I was a baby. The man looked exactly like my
greatgrandfather at twenty, in the pictures I have of him: dark skin,
very dark, dense black hair, the Neapolitan good looks that if you
don't know Naples you want to call sullen.

As I woke up into my babyhood two middle-aged Florentine women sat down between me and the couple. Wealthy Tuscan women: matronly and nicely made up in clear Botticelli colors, dark suits signaling that age has cut them off from high fashion and they know it, but touches like a leopardprint scarf signaling they also know, in a small way, to keep up. They crossed their legs against the couple, who wore bright cheap polyesters with glitter and obviously cut their own hair. Northern Italians hold the south in contempt because it's agrarian and poor and southern people tend to be shorter, squatter and much darker than northerners.

An Italian proverb runs, "Where Naples begins, Africa begins."

The women started talking about the man and woman, loud enough for all of us to hear. They brushed their hands in front of their noses, saying, "What is that fabric?" and *contadini,* "peasants."

It felt odd because in my sleep hangover I had no doubt at all that this was my greatgrandfather. The Florentines treated me politely, all "*mi scusas*" and "*buon giornos,*" though I wore torn cotton pants and had as I often do let my hair tangle for a few days. It didn't matter because Italians view poor dressing as one of Americans' many eccentricities, and the fact that I sat surrounded by books and papers conveyed a sense of social privilege. I had an urge to tap the Neapolitan man on the shoulder and tell him I was going to be his greatgranddaughter. I wanted him to know I'd come back to Italy as a professional, good enough to make Florentines be nice to me. What stopped me wasn't shyness but feeling even half asleep like he might not be that happy, might look right through me and see someone who would put him into words, withholding and changing him.

I can't come to terms with Italy. I went to Barbados and interviewed my family there—I was in college and acted very formal about it, with notebooks—and left with some sense of closure. I learned about the Bajan coffins that dance in their cliffside tombs and the murderous smuggler and my poisoned aunt and many other people and somehow however imperfectly I began to hear them. I've never felt that way about Italy, home of the vague, accidental, duplicable side of my family. It's like the train, when I sat with a man who could have been my greatgrandfather, or for that matter my grandfather, who strongly resembled him, or for that matter my father, who strongly resembled them both. It could have been my grandfather, who's dead, with my infant father in his lap. Though mine in some sense, the man did not look at me. If he had talked to me he might have found me strange and cold—Italians often find Americans so—though I could tell him he had risen like rain through his own pores and fallen, and the woman he looked at now was *la tua nevica*, "your snow."

I write and write in Italy, in Florence, Genoa, Capri, the Cinque Terre, and then throw it all away. More even than in the United States meaning becomes hypercharged, sprinkled everywhere like confetti, which could signify that it passes back into absurdity—or not. Maybe it's a place with not much use for aesthetic subtlety, or maybe it's because the ghosts worry about the obtuseness of an American woman.

We went to the island of Elba and discovered a mountain that like my Barbados greatgreatuncle sinks ships. My greatgreatuncle stole and smuggled rum. He lashed lanterns to trees so they looked like lighthouses and stole the ships' cargo when they sank. The Elba mountain's full of magnetite and draws compass needles so ships go off course and founder. The wrecks have happened since the days of the Phoenicians, though they and the Greeks and Romans and Etruscans went to Elba for mineral-bearing ore—nothing exotic like liquor, just dirt. If you liked symmetry you could say that as they dug out the sides of the mountain to mine it they built it back up from its base in the sea.

Both the mountain and my kinsman stood over while cutters and triremes and whathaveyou, expecting a harbor, sailed straight into rocks, huge carious rocks that split them open and spilt their human cargo into the water. Which closed over them immediately the way language closes over a real event, leaving an unblemished surface.

The name of the Elba mountain, Monte Calamita, can mean either magnet or calamity depending on how it's stressed, one of those double meanings that probably came about not through coincidence but through some longlost metonymy. I saw it in Italian documents printed without accent marks so either meaning could work, and I never asked anyone local to pronounce it.

Guidebooks always translate the name as "calamity" but that's what guidebooks do—make garish meaning for the sake of those who don't have to live with it.

On our way back from Elba the ferry almost sank. Or it seemed to. The ferry crew acted panicked but stoical. We rode through a violent electrical storm and the ferry pitched straight up one way and then the other—a perverse cradle rocking. People fell out of their chairs and got sicker and sicker, and the crew passed out sickness bags printed with serene little swans, though many people couldn't hold out or aim enough to use them. In the middle of the hysteria a woman with a perfectly trained voice, a glorious voice, started singing an aria from Tosca: *"Recondite armonia/di bellezza diversa"*: "the strange harmony of disparate beauties." Enough, I wanted to say, though I was getting sick too. Enough with the gloss on everything, like a caption on a page.

And if you get to the bottom of the sea? Always something with its mouth flapping open, open, open.

———

In 1984 I went with my father to see the village in Italy his family came from, visit his cousins there. A pack of us went—me, Chris, Bruce, my parents, my aunt Philomena. We rented a car and toured around first, oblivious to life back in Toms River—the running raid on Ciba-Geigy, Greenpeace docked in Barnegat Bay. Protestors getting the hell kicked out of them, supposedly by Ciba-Geigy's thugs. My father, Nicola, packed his own toilet paper and worried about traveler's diarrhea and spent the trip obscurely mad at me and my brother. He got incensed at what time we got up and what time we went to bed, what we ordered in restaurants. After a while the sight of us got a snort and a disgusted, "Jeez! You two!" It got so bad my mother did something she rarely does: come in from her distance and play go-between.

"He's driving us nuts," we said to her, in itself a my-fatherly thing to say. In his world things either are nuts or get nuts: "Nuts to that!" And that, and that.

"He just doesn't understand you're not him," my mother said. "You're his kids. He thinks if he's tired, you should be tired."

My relatives lived way up in the mountains, in tiny houses, with handmade clothes that had been patched and patched, so their pants and shirts sang with many fabrics, circles and squares, pockets cut out crudely with pinking shears and tacked on. They said *mulenyans* for eggplant like my father does. They had bad teeth or few teeth though they were lovely people, not metaphorically but really, faces dramatic—flared nostrils and sloped eyes—and beautifully cut. They were small. Most of the men barely reached 5'2", and the women not 5'. At 6' and 5'6" my brother and I seemed enormous.

My father's cousin Vincenzo told him in dialect, "You have big children, but I have grandchildren."

Gesualdo, our village, lies in an earthquake- and volcano-prone region torn up by disaster, disease and war, near Naples and Vesuvius.

Vincenzo showed us buildings and one entire village that had been destroyed by earthquakes, laid out not far from Pompeii like a modern parody of it. The same grid of a town toothed out in foundations, the isolated things some larger humor chooses to keep: where in Pompeii it might be a crumbling caryatid, in Gesualdo I remember a toilet bowl held up on its pipes above the ruins.

"Look at it up there, like it's a king," my father said.

We spent most of our time with Vincenzo, a man wiry and tobaccocolored with wonderfully etched skin, as if an engraver made him. He took us around. In such a neglected place nothing ever gets fixed.

Whatever Vincenzo pointed to he said, *"Terramoto,"* "earthquake," and a word in dialect that meant "destroyed." A landscape of had-beens: a church spire rose behind scaffolding over a ruined church. Old stone crumbled, blocks tilted and moldered. Part of everything remained, the lower, subliminal, nonfunctioning part. A memory of a place.

My dad found everything having to do with his family. We stood together inside the foundations of the cell that had been my father's grandfather's home. It's still there, one room that housed wife, five children and, according to Vincenzo, his goats and chickens in bad weather, until the cholera came.

The houses were cut from stone, bubbly local tufa, each about the size of a college dorm room. What remained of my greatgrandfather's jagged around our knees. I stood there with my father, who brooded under his crowy hair, eyes locked on the soil. We closed the circle of substitutions. My father the grandson whom disaster created, bigger than he should be and me next to him bigger still, with an empty womb. How strange it must have been for those dead, for us to stand there.

I know from family history that the trip across the water, from Naples to Ellis Island, was terrible. Like many things its terribleness never got put in concrete terms, more generalities like heat, crowding, hunger. No one, my parents and aunts and uncles assured me, would do it for themselves. They did it for their offspring, so they could ride the train in torn pants and be respected.

Around Gesualdo the poverty and seismic activity created bad wells. Fever sicknesses passed like a slap from cheek to cheek. Whole towns would die. In America the water came through metal and smelled cleanly of chlorine and no one would have to watch their kids languish in front of them, as they did in Italy, in the flesh.

In the United States my greatgrandfather recreated his life so well he stayed poor. His kids too. My grandfather only got through the fourth grade and worked at miserable jobs like gravedigging. They didn't understand America so when my grandfather a few months before his retirement from a janitor's job was asked to do more and more humiliating things he quit, not realizing he'd lose his pension. My father became an accountant, going to night school when I was a child, and did well. He understood this country though as a father he didn't trust it anymore than his ancestors trusted a village that couldn't even protect itself. He saw raising a child mostly as a struggle against death and sickness, pestilence, disappearing women.

"I am proud to have two such robust children," he once wrote my mother in a letter, with an ineffable air of having searched for that word, "robust."

My family in Italy were plainspoken people. "The Nazis killed twenty-seven here," they'd say, pointing to a field, or to some disaster rubble, "This happened in 1980."

The Italian family in America's this way too.

"Asshole," my father will say of someone he doesn't like, and add,

"He thinks he shits ice cream in three different flavors." In my dad's Brooklynese the "h" of the compound almost disappears, so the "th" words come out close to *t'ink* and *t'ree*.

I have become unintelligible to them, a peddler of metaphor, of veil and the multivalent image. How not? The country I live in is a trope: streets paved in gold, a chicken in every pot, two cars in every garage, the Dream.

We live in our words here and become icons, like poor St. Lucy, with her eyes on a tray in front of her.

A year or so after Halloween, when I hadn't conceived, my doctor suggested fertility treatments.

She said, "It's probably something simple."

Bruce and I spent several years at this, not, in retrospect, for any good reason, but because the problem of our childlessness was always presented as practically solved, with one easy next step. Eggs swelled with Clomid, sperm got centrifuged to make it purer. Most of the steps involved long needles penetrating my cervix. Nothing worked. Still, every month, like a true daughter of my grandmother, I became convinced, after ovulation and whatever monthly tinkering, that I had conceived.

Every month I knew this with a certainty I believed I'd never felt before and would never again feel. I kept my hand on the outside of my womb. I smiled to myself, hummed names, wallowed in the lachrymosity of hormones. Lived from my lap outward: directed Mozart to it, filled my eyes with Caravaggio and thought it down. *The strange harmony of disparate beauties.*

At night I tossed, delivering the news to everybody in long manicky interior conversations.

Hey Bruce Mom Dad Pam Rosina Chris Bobby, I heard myself saying, Guess what . . .

It happened on Valentine's Day, Mardi Gras, Lent, the first day of spring, isn't that the funniest.

We're thinking we'll call her—(Anna May, after my grandmothers. I knew it would be a girl.)

Then on some innocent trip to the toilet I would see that the blood flag had been hoisted again: the first smear of rosy cervical mucus. It was always incredible, a phenomenon I would dismiss for the first few hours as implantation bleeding.

Where the body does offend I needed to see my womb had become a place of drowning and subversion, the cove of the false light, the ancestral home. *Slip its chains & start again*

So many little homicides. How not to hate the waters that could drown them?

Where the body does offend

ask briefly its reason—

In the course of things I had a dye test called a hysterosalpingogram. The test involved radioactive dye squirted up through the cervix and out the fallopian tubes, followed on a monitor. As the dye spread a shape appeared, not a wombshape at all but a shape like a flopped wineskin or a swan drooping its throat to the side. This image appeared on the left side of the screen. The doctor motioned around the darkness on the other side, tracing the same shape.

There's one just like it here, he said, trying not to sound excited. He waved the radiologist in. The radiologist asked him if that one had a viable cervical opening, flicking his eyes at me like he didn't expect me to follow his language. It did not, said my doctor. Nothing got through.

"It's a bicornuate uterus," my doctor told me later. Doublecham-

bered, two identical drooped wineskins with their mouths facing in
opposite directions. One with a cervical opening that accepts dyes and
semens and doctor's tools, one impregnable. Through lovemaking,
my long marriage, miscarriage, it's remained untouched. One chamber has known children and lost children. One has never felt even the
possibility of otherness. A piece of me lodged in my side, beyond the
reach of my life and pointing in a different direction. Even its menstrual flow, its useless ova, must pass back out the fallopian tubes into
the pelvis and be reabsorbed.

Multiplicitous as water: two organs joined by a thin wall living in
two different metaphysical systems, one linear, teleological, organized
by a passage and a monthly liquid purpose: the other circular, time-
thwarting, reabsorbing its end products and starting over again like
the Hindu universe that comes back around on itself. I came to love it,
the inaccessible unlightable chamber defined only by its weaker, more
permeable twin.

In 1896 the X-ray was invented and scientists set about using it to
try to photograph the soul. They never found what they were looking
for, though just what that was I don't know, a bright shape around the
head or the heart I imagine, something obvious we'd all have. Maybe
they never tried looking for the pathology, the blank spot, the secret
bleeding.

If only we could make a language like this, so tangible and full of real
spaces.

I write and write in Italy, and then throw it all away.

Chapter Seven

Trailing Clouds

There was a time when meadow, grove & stream

I was born in the late 1950s. In the afterdin of the McCarthy hearings.
At the start of *To Tell the Truth*, the unfeeling duplicate people of the
Body Snatchers. Into the offcamera bedroom of *The Honeymooners*. In
a country where the dominant species periodically ejected a few of its
members off the surface into space. Then fished them out of the water.
As if we were a panting spaniel of a species using ourselves as balls.

As if we were bored.

We'd dropped two bombs in a place far away and turned two cities
into what looked from the air like two mouths full of serrated teeth.
That was far away and hard to fathom so we decided to make the same

beautiful noises at home, in steel drums surrounded by streams, and use the heat to boil water and light lights.

We built highways then, a big bitumen tic-tac-toe that has taken over much of the work of our raptors—hawks, kestrels, eagles etc.—plump indolent birds now rather than the gaunt kenning things nature made, who wait beside us for the things we flatten. Endangered redtailed hawks stud the highways. Ditto for bald eagles. We wipe out the many and richly stuff the few.

As if we were bored.

It seems we're the only creature that creates such diversions for itself.

My grandfather Louis was in his early forties when he came to Holly Park. My age. I think of him as remote from me, without a life or emotions or a younger man's sexuality, but of course, that can't be true. He had a young family that eddied carelessly around him, and before them he had had less than anyone I can imagine. A mother who left him with strange people in a foreign country. No homeland but four citizenships in a row: British/Bajan, American, Canadian, American. The surname of a man who probably wasn't his father. Brothers and sisters he sounds glad to have seen the last of, except dead Frederick.

Now, in her old age, his mother, Berenda, lives nearby somewhere, maybe with his sister, her namesake, Rennie. Still beautiful, his mother, witchily slim after fourteen children, flesh taut on her sculpted face, her eyes deepset. His mother and his wife, May, each a mystic in her own right, can talk and talk.

He's staying in a tent in Holly Park, on land he razed free of cattails, plotting out where to put the plumbing, the septic tank, using skills no one knows how he acquired. The lagoon exhales its steam of mosquitoes and the bay slumps, up and down, the ratty blue of old corduroy, but still clean. Over the wheaty tops of cattails and the scrub pines he can see the rooftops of a few empty subdivision houses, four years old and peeling.

This space he's chosen for himself isn't downy or sentimental, sweetsmelling or soft. Cattail stubs stick in the back like cut bamboo, beachgrass is whipsharp, the lagoon smells like an old shoe. My grandfather rolls himself up and sleeps, in the malarial music.

He builds the houses with his nephew Kenneth, who drives down for the day, down meandering Route 9 (no Parkway yet), onto the dirt roads. Kenneth's the son of Rennie, who has also spawned Mary and Friend. Rennie's a disgrace to her family, a Catholic convert, full of zeal and devoted to her daughter, Mary, whom she equates with the Virgin. She's always forced both Kenneth and Friend to wait on Mary, take orders from her, and it's wrecked Kenneth's health: he's becoming crippled with arthritis. Friend died in the war. Kenneth's not particularly close to my grandfather but comes and works with him anyway, maybe to get out of the house.

Do they talk, I wonder?

Aside from the bust of the twenties, the area's known for a fabulous killing creature called the Jersey Devil, a thing with batwings and claws and a horselike head.

My grandfather, who along with my grandmother makes no distinctions between the visible and the invisible, the real and the unreal, would have looked for it.

"There it is!" he yells, pointing to a Napoleon's gull. "I see its red eyes."

"She's a Papist," says Kenneth of his mother. "She thinks she eats flesh and drinks blood, every week. The Catholics are taking over New York."

Does Louis still have any of his Creole accent? (I'm thinking of my

Bajan cousin Elizabeth: *See de sea, see? See de sea, see?* A nursery rhyme woman.)

My grandfather sings a song he learned on Barbados.

Shippee fall down, sailor wan go shore

"There'd a not been a war if it weren't for the bloody RCs," says my grandfather, maneuvering his three remaining fingers around the wood.

Back then, just after World War I, it was important to people in America that land be owned. In many places you could just go and buy land for practically nothing or take it and people would say, with a certain measure of relief, that it was yours, you owned it. If you were willing to live on it for a while.

The house goes up, filling with heat and smoke from the potbellied woodstove and cold water from the well. A foamgreen rickety structure built up on pilings. Added later: the humorless grin of the front porch.

The houses become the place where my grandparents practice their spiritualism. My grandmother, aside from her Christian Science, carries the influence of doughty English occultists like Madame Blavatsky, who founded the School of Theosophy in the nineteenth century. Blavatsky believed in the perfectibility of humanity, our ability to become clairvoyant, telekinetic, superhuman. My grandfather had his Bajan beliefs in cursing and divining, and his own beliefs, which excluded religion and standard afterlives but included spirits and ghosts—flitting, bored as he was, in an eternal vacuum.

My grandparents hold séances every weekend and contact a spirit named Simon around a small table. They use their four kids to fill it out. Simon raps out responses, once for yes and twice for no, and uses a Ouija planchette to spell out longer answers.

"What should we name the houses?" my mother, a girl, asks.

Simon spells out *JOURNEY'S END*.

So the houses are still named, with a painted sign out front.

My mother asks who she'll marry, when she'll marry.

Simon is a very physical spirit. He makes the table tip all the way over, dance—shaking up and down on two legs, then the other two—and a handful of times, fly across the room. My mother tells this story:

Their friend the Methodist Reverend Ambrosini is visiting, sitting in a corner by the window (really, my mother says, Ambrosini was a defrocked priest who fled in shame to the Methodists). The Cassills bend around Simon's table, holding hands, asking questions.

"That's godless, dangerous stuff, you know," the Reverend says, and keeps on in this vein: How can you expose your children to demons? Don't you know what is speaking to you?

All of a sudden the table flies across the room, through the air, right at him. Ambrosini spreads backward in horror and tumbles out of his chair and out the window.

Actually my grandmother told me that story first, laughing herself silly. My mother amplifies it. She swears by every detail though she dismisses her family's séances as "that nonsense."

As far as I am concerned being a child happened at Holly Park. Everything else was seeping adulthood.

By common consent, until bedtime, the Little Bungalow belonged to the children. We kept a ladder propped against its side and spent a lot of time crawling around on its almost-flat roof.

The moon hung over us, grail of the sixties, the bloodcup in space. At a bar across the bay we watched the probes land on the moon and Edward White bobbing on his slick umbilicus. The inside of the houses hung almost out of time. Cabbage-rose walls. Kerosene lamps, cold water, sinks and toilets only. The woodstove that leaked oily smoke from its closed mouth. *Life,* Jackie K. with her UFO hats. *Valley of the Dolls.* A teeny almost-toy oven with a pilot you handlit each time you used it.

We would go ten or fifteen years before even replacing wallpaper. Sometimes it took the sight of a baby peeling and eating it in dignified little strips.

My cousin Helen and I washed the family's dishes. Uncle Eddie made us ("Into the kitchen!" one hand on each of our shoulders). We tried to get away before he found us but never did. Kettle after kettle of water put on to boil, a plastic tub filled and emptied and refilled when the water became nauseous with grease and floating scraps.

Our water had an odor like food. It tasted like H_2O pumped from hell's drinking fountain: ten times the legal limit of iron, manganese, a reek of sulfur. We all developed an unaccountable taste for it. Uncle Eddie bottled it and drank it at home.

"Full of good iron," he said.

The Cohansey was full of good iron, good lead, mercury, cadmium, tritium, alpha radiation, good benzenes, PCBs, chlordane, vinyl chloride, lime, mercury, good cyanide.

Through my lifetime the possessed table has squatted in the back bedroom, the one with four bunks where the girls slept. We knew its history. Mark called it "the séance table," and we got the stories from my grandmother and my mother and aunt Kathleen. I haven't slept there in so long my memories are childhood memories, dusted with darkness; I see the room through a haze of slowly clarifying night vision. A battered wooden dresser that humped suspiciously at night. Pale floral wallpaper. A Monty Python poster. Out one window lay the tin trashcan and for a long time an enormous raccoon came each night and got into it—tail and rear in the air like someone had discarded a huge animal—crashing around. It scared me to death.

Lots of things scared me and kept me up at night at Holly Park but not the table, overpainted with blue, though we girls knew Simon shared our room—pentup, with years of answers in him.

I see now the place was a relic of Barbados, almost a parody. The pitched houses isolated, afloat in cattail-fringed tonsure, beyond mail service, unnumbered, on a street that had no name. Between waters, the swampsuck lagoon and the bay, the way the island lay between ocean and sea. We lived like we were on an island. We brought food with us and if it ran out we walked to the nearest grocery a mile and a half away and walked back with supplies in a pullcart. Often we just ate what we could find. We caught crabs and blowfish, picked berries and beach plums. My mother drizzled tapwater into eggs and scrambled them for dinner. No one could afford to change the houses and no one wanted to touch the myth, that we were not a family but a race or a tribe, freshly hacking out our existence. Coming in from the beach at night, mid-1960s, we'd find the Cassill adults sitting in the dark, arguing about Indochina. No one even bothering to light the kerosene. It irritated me.

"We like to talk in the dark," my mother said.

"This family has never needed hot water," my aunt said once.

People Who Speak in Darkness. People Who Shun Hot Water, Dwell on Roof. Eaters of the Water-Egg.

Of course the eggs, and the ham and potato salad and hot dogs full of swinelips (who knew?) and breakfast crullers came from supermarkets in northern New Jersey. And there were other people around, few then more. Users of Little Public Beach. Crabbers off Public Pier. The Schipanos opened their bait and candy store. And the mythical muzzled structure of the Oyster Creek Nuclear Generating Station planted its bones and rose, just a few miles away.

The power plant went up in 1969, built by General Electric from a design created to prove nuclear power plants could be built cheaply. It looked like a giant military barracks with a huge thin smokestack where the emissions the public was promised wouldn't exist could be emitted.

The utility commissioning the plant, General Public Utilities, built a sister plant in Three Mile Island, Pennsylvania.

(On the plant's completion General Public Utilities sued GE. Some said GE workers, shut inside the intestinal tangle of coolant pipes while building, had taken to sending arcs of piss into the core. Also sandwich wrappings and candy bars. "Quite possible," admits the engineer Dale Bridenbaugh, though he doesn't know for sure. However it happened, before the plant began operations, cracks developed around welding in the core. GE settled.)

Oyster Creek the power plant went on to many firsts: record accidents, record radioactive releases.

Willie DeCamp, who founded Oyster Creek Nuclear Watch, emailed me, *The smokestack emanating from the reactor core is not a decoration.*

In the warm water the plant spilled into Oyster Creek the creek, which supplied its cooling water (it enters the plant pure and emerges jazzed with radioactive particles), the creek and its mouth, Barnegat Bay, teemed with strange life.

He added, *In summer the prevailing winds blow toward Holly Park.*

Because of the maze of lagoons, the ground that sobbed under your tread with standing water, mosquito noise droned like modernist music in the summer air. One night I made a quick run across the street in shorts and counted fifty bites when I got back to the Big Cottage. The itch would spread from one bite to another, pulsing over the skin. My cousins and I scratched our legs and arms with a metal hairbrush. Sometimes I poked a pin or a needle into the center of each bite.

When we crouched in the Little Bungalow at night, while the adults sat and rustled in the Big Bungalow, Mark told stories. One started out:

"A man limped down the dirt road to the end when he saw a pair of green houses. With a porch. He limped at the houses, going slower and slower, almost falling, pulling himself up again, pushing up off the ground with his hands. Trying to get to the dim light he saw in the window . . ." Mark had a lot of my grandmother in his storytelling voice—the abstracted look, the pregnant pauses. "But he couldn't. He couldn't make it. In the morning, they found him stretched out on the stairs, dead.

"He was perfectly white. They found . . . all the blood had been drained from his body."

This was the opening of Mark's story of a giant, mutant, killer mosquito. When the power plant went up he added it, saying the mosquito appeared from a pile of nuclear waste.

Because in our hot marshy humid summers it did seem we'd be drained bloodless the DDT truck came around. It chugged down our dirt/gravel road once a week, a boxy thing with pipes that threw out a gray horizontal cloud. Sometimes a small cropdusting plane came instead, light and twisting just above the cottages. Whichever, we called it just the Sprayer.

"Sprayer! Sprayer!" the women in the family would shout. "The cats!"

My mother and aunts slammed the windows shut and dragged the cats in. For some reason they related the danger of pesticides to animals, not children, not Baby Boom children. We were somehow not human. (So many kids around parents resorted to elaborate ornamentation: Tony Home Permanents, dresses that made girls look like petits fours, boys in caps and sailor suits.)

My cousins and I chugged along behind the DDT truck, drawn by the pluming tailfins.

The smoke, lupine in color, hung in the air and then began meandering to the left and right in an almost articulate way, like a tail being wagged. It scorched our mouths and noses and that night we would sit together and eat food we could not taste. No one gave chemicals a second thought until the late sixties, early seventies: and by then we were dropping burning jellied gasoline on Vietnamese villagers.

As I said, we caught blowfish, a smallish gray fish that ballooned when touched. We gutted them, fried them, ate white petals of meat off the bone. We had them several times a week, and crab, gummed into crabcakes. Blowfish are tough fish—scavengers, able to survive in almost any kind of water.

In 1952, at the height of McCarthyism, the year of Mark's birth and four years before mine, the Ciba-Geigy company built its plant along Toms River, four miles or so west of our cottages. The Ciba-Geigy site took up 1,400 acres—cleared areas, pine barrens and wetlands—and shaped into a constellation of plants where it manufactured its dyes, pigments, resins and epoxies. It's a lovely spot in many ways, even when the men from the government in their white suits with bubble masks were there, scooping the soil and groundwater into little cups. A place of dwarf pines, weeping white cedars, creeks,

> a buried drum disposal area containing 31,000 drums; a 160,000 cubic yard lime sludge disposal area containing a high percentage of inorganic wastes; a 12 acres filtercake disposal area containing wastewater treatment sludge; five backfilled lagoons which total 8½ acres; a 25 acre area contains construction and demolition debris, scattered chemical wastes . . .
>
> Groundwater and soils are contaminated with volatile organic

compounds including benzene, trichloroethylene, chlorobenzene, 1, 2-
dichloroethane and toluene as well as heavy metals including arsenic
and chromium.

groundwater and soils pose a public health hazard if ingested or
touched. *(EPA, from the site report)*

The EPA gives us our diarists, our cataloguers, even our poetry:
Homers of this century's misadventures.

An elementary school is located adjacent to the site along the south-
western fence

The groundwater plume is migrating to the Toms River and wetlands
along the east

In my one brief pregnancy my list of forbidden foods included
most of the seafoods I grew up on, crab and bottomfeeding fish; they
scavenge and eat and store toxins in their fatty tissues. My aunt Kathleen dimly remembers a time when Barnegat Bay ran with red snap-
per and flatfish; we still occasionally caught fluke when I was little.
Mostly my mom and my aunts and uncle grew up on blowfish like we
did, and crab and berries censed with DDT.

When you find them Double do not meddle with them
for they are Deformed; Nature cannot any longer
live among the Monsters & the mutilated

I was born in the 1950s, in the forty-year U.S. public relations move
called the Cold War; I was born with a womb with two sealed chambers. Because one side lacked any cervical opening, when puberty
came its menstrual blood flowed retrograde, back through the fallopian tube, sprayed lazily through the pelvis, where it left lush patches

of endometrial tissue. My one pregnancy, naturally occurring quad-ruplets, miscarried. By the time I was thirty my thyroid swelled with tumors, swans' eggs in my throat. Bits of these have been carefully fanned out along a slide. They're thyroid cells, with their DNA damaged so they don't know how to do their jobs anymore and just keep reproducing.

We are the Roof Dwellers, the People Who Speak in Darkness; we're also the DDT People, the Drink-Cadmium People, the Breathing-Isotope People.

Our early clouds of glory were otiose balloons of dichlorodiphenyl-trichloroethane, probably the most famous pesticide used in America. Also one of the most persistent. DDT was originally praised for this quality but after a while its persistence started getting on nerves, like a vacuum cleaner salesman who days later is still showing you model after model and throwing sawdust on your carpet. In the body DDT behaves hormonally, like an estrogen, disrupting endocrine signals. It damages the liver, acts as a carcinogen, causes seizures. It does not leave the body but metamorphoses and nests in fatty tissue as its alter ego DDE. When a pregnant woman begins the work of forming her infant she will draw on her fat reserves; I mean to say, her DDE reserves.

PCBs, dioxins, chlordane, are also endocrine disruptors: all spilled in our area.

> Maternal animals, including humans, store
> endocrine-disrupting agents in their
> fat prior to reproduction, then mobilize
> these agents during periods of egg laying, pregnancy or
> lactation

There may occur immediate or latent adverse effects on the offspring that are likely to be irreversible.

(EPA Special Report on Environmental Endocrine Disruption: An Effects Assessment and Analysis, 1997)

The highest concentration of DDE in an exposed mother will be found in her breastmilk. Unlike most 1950s women, and unlike herself, with her horror of things physical, my mother breastfed.

I am a little World made Cunningly
Of Elements and an angelick Sprite

And our bards sing to us of babies at the breast, how it can mean the end of their developmental and reproductive soundness, with misformed reproductive organs, endometriosis and more. How delicate it all is.

I'm the product of my mother and father's DNA and of their DDE: these lay down with them in the nuptial chamber. A mouthful of breastmilk and DDE formed my first human meal. At the resurrection of the body we will carry these along with our sins to the throne of judgment. Peter will weigh them: sins, graces, pesticides, radiation.

At the end of the twentieth century comes our human seachange, to longlived shadow creatures. When the creek runs through the power plant it emerges radiated; permissible leak levels for a nuclear power plant are ten gallons a minute for its coolant body. Its smokestack vents steam laced with radioactive particles. Some radioactive substances go through a brief filtering process now, and some like tritium are unfilterable so releasing them is legal. Tritium, actually radioactive hydrogen, becomes part of the water in your body, which becomes tritiated water. Instead of 70% H_2O you become 70% $3H_2O$. You will be tritiated for somewhere between one hundred days and ten years. So many fission products, like strontium-90, are boneseekers—

chemically so like calcium your body stores them in bones and teeth—
that some Ocean County teeth click under the radiation counters of
the baby teeth project.

The industry rule: ALARA. As Low As Reasonably Achievable

Xenon, another release, decays into cesium, an isotope with a half-
life of three million years; it will take three million years to become
half as radioactive. Plutonium has a half-life of twenty-four thousand
years. It stirs in tiny quantities in our sludge. Because radioactive particles are looking for electrons to stabilize themselves they will nest in
the cells of any body consuming or inhaling them. They infiltrate
DNA and resequence it. With cesium and plutonium and tritium fret-
ted into our DNA we gain a grotesque, exhausted immortality, a race
of Cumaean sibyls.

At extensive dumpsites like Ciba-Geigy, radioactive particles used
in chemical processes lie side by side with heavyduty pesticides like
chlordane. One of the epiphanies of Rachel Carson's book *Silent
Spring* was the extent to which radiation and chemical contamination
increase each other's effects when they're found in the same area,
working in similar ways to attack cell structure and DNA, and deacti-
vating the body's defenses. Like the radiation and chemotherapy treatment we use for aggressive cancers, directed at the healthy body.

The developer of DDT, Paul Hermann Muller, won the Nobel Prize
for it in 1948. After World War II, along with communism (men drag-
ging home with malaria) the United States declared war on insects. A
popular floorwax had pesticide worked into it, so the floor itself could
destroy any little creeping thing. Paul Muller doesn't seem to have
worried about the applications of DDT. He did go on to become an
apocalyptician of nuclear fission, though, declaring it would in some
form end the world.

———

When my father came down the shore on weekends (from industrial Elizabeth) he liked to breathe deeply and say, "Oh the fresh air. It just makes you sick."

The air did smell briny fresh, between DDT sprayings, with a wheaty underodor of cut cattail. Our parents said, "We are getting away from it all."

In the end Holly Park did form a sanctuary. It was my and my cousins' world. There was the gravelly road that turned the sound of cars into a long drag so we knew when family was coming. The sweet poisoned fish. We always had a girls' fort and a boys' fort stomped out of the cattails next to the houses, so we could play war, in our helmets and clutching plastic bayonets.

School made a nine-month chafe, Huck Finn's sivilizing stay with the Widow Douglas. One place with one view and one voice snoring in your ear. The extent to which we kids did whatever we wanted to do at the shore seems astonishing in retrospect. My father worked and could only come down the shore on weekends. My mother was a helpless disciplinarian, not softhearted but lacking in focus. At the shore she wore slacks and no lipstick and folded herself onto the sofa with books and magazines; she reverted in her childhood home to some earlier form of herself. She became inert, a noble gas.

Every few hours she used to poke her head out the door and say, "Kids. Whatever you're doing, you probably shouldn't be doing it."

Or she said, "Don't get any bright ideas."

My mother called all bad behavior having "bright ideas." Or "big ideas." It was her ultimate warning, not to think. "I'm leaving now but don't get any big ideas!" Flooding the beach was a *bright idea*.

My mom referred all disciplinary matters to my father anyway, who yelled himself purple and hung over us children the way he hung over the engine of our fatiguegreen Dart when it broke down: furious and confused. At home in Elizabeth he devised punishments of weeks alone in your room, no toys or books. He relaxed his guard at the shore. A Navy man, he taught us kids poker, no wild cards, stud or draw only.

My parents made a lot of jokes about the nuclear power plant.

"We'll all be roasted in our beds," my mother liked to say. She had that kind of fifties humor: black but very cheerful. She made it sound like being roasted in your bed was perfectly fine. She had the fifties vocabulary too: *roasted, toasted, glowing, burned to a crisp.* Not *nuked,* a newer word.

While they thought about being roasted we kids did what we wanted to do. My cousin Mark had a tiny sailboat we sailed way past the sight of land. It capsized if you misstepped and was unrightable, so when it did capsize you had to flag down a motorboat to tow you in.

Mark bossed us all around because he was the oldest, and anyway, he was naturally bossy. Helen and I got to boss the other girls, for the same reason.

Mark would say, "We're going to make bombs." Three or four of us would get the job of scraping the tips off hundreds of matches into pouches of aluminum foil.

Then Mark would say, "We're going to get Hanoi." Some part of the house, say the kitchen with its rustcreased linoleum, would be designated Hanoi. At the touch of a match his foil bombs flew across the room.

Once we found in the lagoon a spent shell, a two foot long khaki missileshaped thing, blown in from some military training exercise or maybe an offshore skirmish.

"Neat."

"This is the neatest." (That was the word then.)

We carried it to the Little Cottage and kept it propped up outside and pretended to shoot it at one another. We hit it with hammers, thinking that in everything like that—khaki, serious, utilitarian—there was a splendid fire buried deep.

We believed for a long time it was a nuclear missile. We planned our mushroom cloud, that shape we saw all the time on television and admired, stalked, crowned and growing out from the top: a spit in the face of gravity. We knew there were nuclear bombs in the last war and we knew people were experimenting with nuclear power, one of the first experiments a few miles from the Big Bungalow and the Little Cottage. I believed the roof of the nuclear power plant capped a mushroom cloud that would one of these days curl from a carelessly opened window, from that long low building on Oyster Creek in Forked (two syllables) River.

We played nuclear war and imagined the outcome, pulling at our hair and squishing our faces into pictures of running flesh.

My blurring of fission power and fission weapons had a historical logic. Nuclear power evolved from the bomb, the "new control" over nature I. I. Rabi described, the "Birth of the World" William Laurence rhapsodized about—both men involved in the bomb's creation. The forties and fifties spawned a litter of utopian writing about nuclear fission—it would be humankind's *new fire*, a process the scientist J.B.S. Haldane said could save civilization, if not destroy it.

Dyson Carter, an engineer and nuclear power advocate, wrote in a 1946 pamphlet called "Atomic Dollars":

Eventually our cities can be warmed in winter by small suns put up along the streets in much the same way as we hang street lights. Comfortable radiant heat from a sun on every corner will not only keep our houses warm but also take the chill off a January blizzard outdoors, melt the snow as soon as it falls, give us cheerful and healthful sunshine on cloudy or rainy days, and dispel the gloomy darkness of long winter nights. You could get a baking hot sun-bath sitting on your back porch in the middle of February.

This was an optimism in refashioned weapons the young of Vietnam could never accept.

It's hard to pose these children, playing fallout around their spent shell, against the Cassill adults at Holly Park. Who cooked baked beans on the woodstove and closed windows against the clouds of DDT. They moved slowly and lazily behind half-closed blinds, in the spirit of the cattails and high fat cumulus.

To them the children blurred. The young of the tribe, the Boys and the Girls. We all got blamed for stuff, or none of us did. I had the experience of my parents confusing me not just with my brother, but with my cousins. Slinging along the Garden State Parkway, four distinct heads in the metal bucket of a Dodge Dart, tabby cat in cardboard, we drove from the view of multiple paint factories in Elizabeth to the view of the singular, slightly agitated bay. We drove from Mother, Father, Sister, Brother, into One Ofdom.

So the young grew different in secret. Mark studied *The Rise and Fall of the Third Reich* and played Nazi. He introduced us younger kids to de Sade. My cousin Helen ate in high school and starved in college, till she was sick. I used drugs.

Of course we never talked about these things. When I was little my mother's English cousin Mary visited us a lot; I remember her unbelievably smooth redlacquered fingernails, which I used to stroke and bite. I loved her for the way she pronounced "anything": *ennathing*. Then she moved in with her boyfriend and we refused to let her come and pretended she'd never existed.

"Trash bum!" my uncle Eddie would say if he heard her name, and throw something down. That was it. We never discussed her.

My mother would say of someone we'd cut off, "We just don't hold with that."

If prodded she'd specify what by saying, "You know. That."

My family has what they call Family Councils. My aunt called one recently to announce her daughter Melinda's divorce, to explain that the circumstances were clean, no shenanigans or other men. She didn't want her family to declare her daughter dead.

My mother, small and sharpfeatured, sharpvoiced: sometimes she tells me if I left my husband she'd never want to see me again. Sometimes she sews me little table napkins of dotted cotton. Her arthritis is bad now; she needs me to chop onions and peppers for her and leave them in her freezer.

She calls her West Indian family "British." The Cassills pretend to be monoracial though it's clear from looking at pictures of my great-grandparents that we're not. As children Helen and I had a sadistic sense of their anxiety. "Your hair is looking awfully nappy today," we'd tell my aunt Kathleen, the sensitive sister, who'd skittle off to a mirror.

"I don't know about you Susanne," is my mother's favorite thing to say.

At thirteen, in the 1969 of the moon landing, the Newark and Elizabeth riots, the power plant, the year after the deaths of Bobby Kennedy and Martin Luther King and the Summer of Love, I discovered marijuana and hashish, speed, downs and acid, mescaline and peyote. Richard Nixon's law-and-order platform had carried the 1968 election, and Operation Intercept held up the flow of marijuana from Mexico to the United States, though the one clear marijuana danger came not from the plant but a pesticide used to spray it—paraquat. I had DDE in my fatty tissues, lead and mercury, dioxins, PCBs, iodine-131, strontium-90 loading in the bones. I was $3H_2O$.

I used drugs heavily and pretty much quit going to school by 1970, the year the Cuyahoga River near Cleveland got so brined with chemical ooze the river itself went up in flames.

As marijuana swept the country—its mystique fueled by Operation Intercept's shortage—kids thought of names for it: weed, grass. What it did: buzzed, ripped.

"I'm really fucking toasted," kids said.

When I was fifteen with the onset of Watergate came cocaine and the great love of my drug life, narcotics. Heroin, methadone, dilaudid. It wasn't just what I used but the Grand Guignol of the combinations—three tabs of acid, four Quaaludes, joints soaked in hash oil, vodka. A nostril for heroin, a nostril for coke. I dropped out of school. In the early seventies I learned language again. Stuff or shit, pigs, dudes, bitches.

My boyfriend introduced me by saying, "This is my bitch."

My boyfriend Kenny and I rode to the shore on his Harley-Davidson, crashing along at eighty or ninety, all fucked up. My body had become pointless, not something to relish moving through the water but something to spring off from into another place.

"Christ! I'm so ripped I don't remember getting here," we said all the time.

From my years of drug use I have images, pictures without narrative. I can't recall much but I have diaries from this time—long elaborate entries—so I can at least remember remembering. And I have moments: Kenny and I roaring off from Holly Park to the amusement park at Island Beach, on blotter acid, riding the Centrifuge. Him pulling over to let me puke. I passed out many times on the sofa of the Big Cottage and feel that still—burlapy cheekscrape fabric, rustred, scented with a little mildew. People shook me awake in the morning.

No Family Councils, no shunnings in that Amish manner. Because my behavior was inarticulable, because it involved silence and secrecy and happened like race in the bloodstream, I was somehow safe. My cousins dragged the unspeakable into their domestic spaces. I admitted nothing.

In 1972, a narcotics year, the Atomic Energy Commission charged a group of its people with studying pressure suppression containment nuclear reactors like the one at Oyster Creek—the same class of design used at Chernobyl in Russia. The report recommended they be phased out. The agency dismissed the report, and the *New York Times* ran a blistering story accusing the AEC of covering up.

My parents looked at me sometimes then and said, "We don't know what to do with you."

Maybe I was Shaman, Voice from the Other Side.

That same year, a pain cut through the haze for a while. It got so bad I couldn't ride the motorcycle, not even drugged up with Quaaludes or heroin. In my lower pelvis two precise points on either side of the groin burned like a twisted sac of matchheads or a prophet's coals. The jouncing of the bike roused them to fire. I finally got myself to a gyno, who noted but didn't mention the cigarette burns and glass cuts on my arms. As soon as he went in to start the pelvic exam I screamed in pain. I had enormous cysts on my ovaries.

"Rare in somebody your age," he said. After months of hormone therapy they dissolved.

In the twenty-five years since, the growths have come back and back. Into the nineties, the decade of ozone and spotted owls and EPA reports on the effects of DDT, radiation, chemical wastes on the body. Once it took major surgery to remove them, during which the docs paddled around, fascinated, in my double uterus. The growths are back now. Endometrial tissue, wild luteal tissue. That burning pain, which you also could compare to hot needles.

A body that doesn't know when to quit. Quite literally.

Structural abnormalities of the uterus and oviducts,
reproductive dysfunction
nonneoplastic lesions such as parovarian cysts

have been associated with prenatal exposure
Endocrine disruptors may act as hypertrophic (stimulatory)
agents
and tumor promotors
target organs include the liver and the thyroid
(*EPA Special Report on Environmental Endocrine Disruption: An Effects
Assessment and Analysis, 1997*)

Every two or three years I've had to have my thyroid tumors biop-
sied. They're what doctors call "suspicious," being actual thyroid tissue that can't stop reproducing. They get bigger and bigger, the kind
of growths that often become cancer.

In the late seventies, after I cleaned up, I took courses at a community
college and finally transferred to a four-year school. At the end of my
junior year I went down the shore with my parents: early May 1979.
Car travel had become a luxury as the gas crisis grew and gas stations
ran out. We'd wait in line for several hours to get the gas to drive down
the shore. Gas prices doubled and nuclear power soared in popularity.
    I remember my father waiting at the gas station, on lines that coiled
for blocks and blocks. It had become the rule that you couldn't fill up
unless you were below half a tank. My dad hates to let his gas gauge go
below half and this rule, as well as the waiting, drove him crazy. He
fidgeted, moved his hands loudly from one position on the steering
wheel to another, sighed, twisted the radio dial before snapping it off.

"Christ! It's all a buncha crap."

He'd threaten not to go ("Nuts! It's not worth it") then look around guiltily.

I swam at the shore and caught up on sleep.

While I did, a pressure spike on the reactor switches, combined with one pump already out of commission due to seal problems, caused the circulating water at Oyster Creek to stop flowing. The reactor core fissioned on without any fresh cooling water to channel and control the heat. The water around the core, unreplenished, turned to steam in seconds in the phenomenal heat.

The water level protecting the fissioning core dropped from fourteen feet to, perhaps, one. The core got hot, hotter, too hot. Radioactivity spewed into the atmosphere, four or five times the amount that had been recently dumped by the accident at Three Mile Island. It contributed to 1979's record release of radioactivity at Oyster Creek, around a million curies for the year.

I'd wiped myself out at school, routinely writing papers three or four times the required length, sure I'd fail. I loved the chance to sleep.

After I quit using drugs I spent years worrying about what I might have done to myself. If nothing else the hundreds of acid trips, the narcotics ODs, seem like they would have smothered something.

Though I have malformed reproductive organs, tumors, weird botched pregnancies and more, as it turns out my five female cousins, who as teenagers made Honor Roll and ironed their hair and learned cheers, fall apart in as many intricate ways. As children, even in the womb, we changed, charged and reformed by the landscape. I may have pummeled away at my central nervous system and organs and drifts of ganglia but what did it was the small white fish and the blackberries and the air itself.

In the 1980s both Mark and I were diagnosed with manic-depressive disorder and put on lithium, one of the chemicals Ciba-Geigy was spilling, along with ninety-eight others, into the water and the soil.

Our parents are the products of the Depression. My father grew up very poor; his father mostly out of work and my dad working at age ten, selling magazines and whatnot, to put food on the table. A signal phrase with him, one that enfolds all motivation and desire. To put food on the table. To put *food* on the *table.* He lived on a floor of a brownstone in Brooklyn, three or four rooms, a family of four kids eating white beans and bread. I come from immigrants, people who pointed their fingers to the United States on maps when they lived in places where this country was inconceivable. And said, here my children and grandchildren can do better.

My Bajan grandfather continued his job—selling insurance for the Prudential—through the Depression, but his family had to take in boarders to make ends meet.

Our parents loved the future. The fifties and sixties were a bright shining place. They did not believe they had just fifteen years. They believed in progress and an end to bugs and a cloud of prosperity that would lift itself free of the earth's resources and expand and expand and rain down.

They wanted to give their children the gift of open spaces.

My father had seen his younger brother almost die of scarlet fever and his mother die young of a heart scarred by rheumatic fever and poor postpartum care. He wanted us to be healthy. He took us to swim, or my mother did, every day.

My mother wanted us to carry forward her family, that oddly transplanted colonial family from the tropics, the love of roofs and cold water and kerosene straining into the twenty-first century.

They do not believe in things psychological and feel that now in the nineties we make too much of stuff. Trauma. Global warming. They went from being sixties Democrats to nineties conservative Republicans. They're sick of what we Baby Boomers do, sharing and encountering, dithering and blathering. They hate abortion.

"Think of all those parents waiting for a baby," says my dad, who should know.

My parents also hate that I'm researching DDT and the power plant and the dumpsites.

"Why bother? You'll never know for sure what's wrong with you," my father says.

"We gave you," says my mother, "everything we had." And put food on the table, always.

Postscript: 1976

February 2, 1976
Mr. N. L. Felmus
Manager, BWR Services
General Electric Company
175 Curtner Avenue
San Jose, California

Dear Neil:

This letter is to advise you that I am resigning from the General Electric Company effective immediately.

My reason for leaving is that I have become deeply concerned about the impact environmentally, politically, socially and genetically that nuclear power has made and potentially can make to life on earth. As we have discussed in the past, there is an inherent close intertie between commercial power and weapons technologies and capabilities. I am strongly opposed to the deployment of such capabilities and I fear the implications of a plutonium economy. The risk involved in such a system is far too great for the short term benefit. I see no way for us to develop the ability to maintain the perfect human and technical control needed for the long periods of time necessarily involved with the highly toxic materials we are producing. This problem is not something I wish to pass on to my children and to succeeding generations to control. Contributing to the advancement of such proliferation now seems immoral and is no longer an acceptable occupation for me.

Furthermore, in my recent assignment as the Project Manager of the Mark I Containment assessment, I have become increasingly alarmed at the shallowness of understanding that has formed the basis for many of the current designs. It is probable that many more problems will emerge with severe consequences, impacting either the safety or the economic viability of the nuclear power program.

It is hard for the mind to comprehend the immensity of the power contained in the relatively small reactor core and the risk associated with its control. In the past we have been able to learn from our technological mistakes. With nuclear power we cannot afford that luxury!

Much has been entrusted to the corporate and regulatory decision makers and the tremendous cost, schedule, and political pressures these humans experience have made unbiased decisions, with true evaluation of the consequences, very difficult to achieve. This is not meant as an indictment of any specific individuals; it is just a statement of the human imperfection which leads, ultimately, to the imperfection of the complex technological system. Nuclear power has become a technological monster and it is not clear who, if anyone, is in control.

In summary, I am no longer convinced of the technical safety of nuclear power and I fear the high risk of political and human factors that will ultimately lead to the misuse of its byproducts. This makes it impossible for me to work in an objective manner in my current position and I, therefore, have decided that my only choice is to get out of the nuclear business. This seems the only course of action for me to take if I am to be fair to my associates, the Company, to you, and to myself.

I also must tell you that I have become so convinced that nuclear power is not right for this country or for this world, that I have decided to volunteer my time for the next several months to work in support of the California Nuclear Safeguards Initiative. Following this, I will be looking for a job either in a non-nuclear area or, if possible, where I can use my experience to help safeguard the substantial nuclear legacy that has already been created.

I am sorry that I have been unable until now to fully confide in you the concerns I have had. This has not been an easy decision for me to make, but I finally came to the conclusion that it is something I must do. Perhaps my action will cause other people to consider the vast implications of the nuclear power program before it is too late.

I have come to believe very deeply that we cannot afford nuclear power and I intend to do whatever I can to get the message to the public where the decision on its continuation must ultimately be made.

> Sincerely,
> Dale G. Bridenbaugh
> Manager, Performance Evaluation and Improvement
> Manager, Mark I Containment Program

Chapter Eight

The Jersey Devil

My family would count this scene as a beginning, maybe arbitrarily—of itself, an entity, an animal with its own hungers and demands: my grandfather Louis sleeping in a tent on his land in Ocean County, at the edge of the Pine Barrens where the Jersey Devil, a thirteenth child like my grandfather, killed and mutilated chickens and sheep and dogs and cattle and, my family said, babies, though I can't find stories like that in the books.

Though the Jersey Devil was born in 1735, the 2,000 square miles of

Pine Barrens in southeastern New Jersey disturbed the Lenni-Lenape Indians so much they rarely went in there, even before. It would have been a place waiting for a monster, just as Lourdes with its bubbling waters waited for its Mary. People compare the Barrens to Eastern Europe, to something from an Eastern European folktale. It is a place where the colors and sizes of nature seem to have become unstuck. Rivers like the Mullica and the Batsto run tannic red, bloody, not the freshly oxygenated blood of arteries but the brackish emptied blood of menses or of veins. Many of the forests are dwarf forests built on sandy soil—troll-like stands of stunted pitch pines where for centuries people have fled to hide, smugglers and traitors and murderers, though a man standing a hundred yards away from you would be clearly visible there, a human hairline at the tops of the trees. Like a child hiding plain under a bedsheet.

Though botanists have studied and speculated no one knows why the forests in the Barrens grow so small.

Flowers have names like pitcher plant, sparkle, whippoorwill shoe. The area had several brief booms but mostly has remained isolated and poor, at least in the interior, with inhabitants called pineys who've been there for centuries.

My cousin Mark always told us pineys inbred, produced troglodytes—pale hairless but recognizably Neanderthal children—and practiced cannibalism. My father and my uncle drove us deep into the Barrens and Mark showed us the eyes rustling behind low leaves of huckleberry.

He had stories that began with a car broken down and a crazy piney in the weeds.

"They were driving along, a normal family, three kids in the back, two boys and a girl. The engine coughed and sputtered and then—it died. It died dead. And there was a sound like a squirrel only bigger than a squirrel . . . "

The Barrens are essentially a bog, a layer of shifting sand over an aquifer that covers a million acres, and the water mixed with tannin and iron runs in the rivers and bubbles up into boglands. The main products of the Barrens have been bog crops like cranberries and, at one time, bog iron, and other bog things like smuggling, things that thrive in a place where the main event courses below the surface.

My grandfather like the Jersey Devil was an abandoned thirteenth. He may not have been abandoned as emphatically as the Devil but his mother put even more distance between her and him, leaving him in the States to go back to Barbados whenever she felt like it, and unlike the Devil's mother she victimized his siblings as well.

Given my family's history my greatgrandmother may have known something of motherly negligence, though I guess the Devil's mother, Mother Leeds, could make the same claim, a woman with twelve children underfoot, who maybe cursed her baby herself, maybe was raped, maybe was raped by the devil in the guise of a pirate, maybe had a liaison with an English soldier during the Revolutionary War (if you accept a different birthdate) and was cursed by townspeople as a traitor.

(Mostly Tories—English sympathizers—settled the Barrens anyway; they went into the low woods to hide after the redcoats ran and were joined by Hessian soldiers who didn't want to leave. We forget our Revolutionary War had two sides, and one side wept over portraits of mad George and crept into the trees.)

My grandfather may have been the son of the man he called his father, or he may have been fathered during one of his mother's periodic jaunts living at the local military garrison, sleeping with the soldiers. He may have left Barbados as a boy or as a teenager, may have gone back a lot, or not till his thirties. He disappeared for several years as a young man and turned up in Canada, maybe in trouble with the law, maybe as my cousin says just afraid of his mother.

Ah, myth.

It startled me when I realized, looking at a New Jersey map, that Holly Park is part of the Pine Barrens. We thought of the Barrens as distant, or at least other, a wild scrub of traitor and troglodyte, all the more awful for its childsized incoherence. This though Holly Park has the sand soil and cattails and pine and white cedar landscape of the Barrens, and water moving under us tasted palpably of iron when pumped, as if forced up through the barrel of a gun.

And for a fact my grandpa had a bit of the piney about him. He knew how to brew his own root beer and we children had to dig him the sassafras roots, from saplings only, so we searched the woods for the low trinity of leaves, three-frond, two-frond and one-frond together on one branch, and sucked some of the roots we dug for their starchy rootbeer flavor. When we fished Barnegat Bay we often drew eels into the boat; they writhed like full gospel people on the bottom of our dinghy and the rest of us threw them back but my grandfather loved to eat them and hung them, skinned, in our kitchen, like soft bloody ropes.

My grandfather's piney spirit built our houses and sank our well. Living over an aquifer pineys supposedly know water and can always tap into it, the ground of their being.

The Jersey Devil has the head of a horse or a ram or a collie dog, gigantic batwings, a crane's legs, hooves and a short tail. It can tear cows,

German shepherds and sheep limb from limb and is most known for its eldritch scream, half laugh but tinged with horror, and the little cloven prints it leaves running across fields and roofs. It flies and still appears regularly around the Barrens. In the most common nativity story Mother Leeds willed her thirteenth child to the devil because she had too many and the child was transformed at birth into the devil's spawn. It flew out her window, some say after stopping to devour Mother Leeds and the other Leeds children.

The Jersey Devil loves our coast, the coast of Barnegat. He's always amused himself by sitting in trees looking out for sinking ships to laugh at.

The pirate Captain Kidd also loved our coast. He's supposed to have stashed his riches along Barnegat Bay, chests of starred sapphires and gold pieces and fine brandies, and we used to play at digging for it in our lagoon. Captain Kidd buried his loot and, following the custom among pirates—who only feared the dead—beheaded one of his best men and left the corpse there to protect his treasure. The headless pirate and the Devil became fast friends and walked the shore together through the centuries, seen by many, in profile a sharpwinged horse-headed one, and one stopped at the neck who nevertheless managed to give an air of rumination. If the dead pirate liked to laugh at shipwrecks too it could only be seen in his hands.

Our Big Bungalow, which was built maybe thirty yards from the bay and so sounded like the interior of a face being lightly slapped, day in, day out, had a screened porch we used at times for sleeping. Originally the house stopped at the door to this porch and my grandfather clapped the room on later, basically just three walls of screens with a door and two ancient and very mildewed sofabeds for Helen and me, when younger girls displaced us from our back bedroom.

Helen, fearless and practical, went to bed by announcing she was tired, diving down in a t-shirt and going instantly into a comalike sleep. I went to bed when she did and lay there thinking of excuses to wake her.

I hated sleeping on that porch. Mosquitoes droned in its shadows waiting to dive the soft cuffs of our ears. Worse, some nights when I slept there or tried to sleep, I heard a rhythmic tread around the house, someone circling close to the cottage, chillingly slow, slowing even more at our windows. I never opened my eyes. It didn't scare me so much that someone walked around the house—Holly Park and my family had more than their share of oddballs—as that obsessive but almost hesitant pace and my family's presence around the table in the morning, bright, chipper and uninterested. I couldn't get anyone to listen to my stories of the walker, though if the night was dry I'd find footprints and offer to show them.

It's a sampler of Americana, people who've seen the Jersey Devil over time: Joseph Bonaparte, Napoleon's brother, on a shooting trip in the Barrens. Captain Kidd. Commodore Stephen Decatur, hero of the War of 1812, the man who coined the phrase "my country, right or wrong," who sailed up to the Hanover Iron Works to check the progress of his cannonballs during a war with the Barbary Coast pirates. Decatur, who must have been a levelheaded man, shot a cannon at the thing but it flew on carelessly with a hole in its middle. Innumerable mayors, policemen, city councilmen, reverends, the entire Black Hawk Social Club in Riverside, and the West Collingswood Fire Department have reported sightings; the Collingswood firemen even turned their hoses on it in 1909.

In 1740 a priest rustled his soutane into the Barrens and exorcised the Devil by bell, book and candle. The exorcism, he warned, would last only one hundred years. And indeed the creature came back around 1840, scattering sheep entrails and laughing.

Like his thirteenth child kindred my grandfather found many bad things funny. Wars irritated but amused him. He cackled at the story of his greatuncle the wrecker and smuggler. When men came to his door with Bibles or Mormon tracts he ran and got his Christian Scientist wife and stood back in the shadows, laughing, as she lectured them.

For us in the bay side of Ocean County, Island Beach formed our other side of the tracks, with its ruffling water, silky sand and miles of swelling dune. My grandfather claimed that all of Island Beach clumped up as the result of a hurricane and that he could remember when it happened and when Holly Park stood at oceanfront. I think that was a lie.

Island Beach had boardwalk amusement parks like Seaside and rows of nouveau tony vacation towns like Lavalette, houses in baby colors of pink and blue and yellow and carefully fenced sand yards with driftwood placed like shrubs. The Atlantic would rock you like a mother gone nuts; we loved it. Island Beach represented New Jersey's desirable shore while Barnegat served as the working people's water, a place for subsistence dwellers and the cheapest summer cabins and for northern and southern state industries to dump their chemical wastes. A good spot to choose for trying out a budget nuclear power plant.

Barnegat, in my lifetime and much of my mother's, was a filthy water. Not only do our towns like Holly Park and Toms River top the nation in rates of leukemia and cancer but the water itself breeds strange and luxuriant flora, kelp wigs pearled with barnacle, lungs and kidneys and brains of seaweed, as if we stood above a great dissection room. Stepping into our bay was like stepping into a pot of mutant spinach. Consequently, though we had nothing but sand soil in Holly Park, we had no real sand beaches that I knew of; the tiny beach across the street from our house had wooden barriers erected against the water, with thickly mossed stairs to climb down into it. No one wanted the water to meet the land, lapping that stuff at our feet.

Barnegat also grew shipworms after the nuclear power plant moved in: like termites in water, they eat wood. Across the bay dinghies and piers would bob with a certain insouciance, bottomless.

Because of the Jersey Devil our stretch of south Jersey was called by the Native Americans "Popuessing," or place of the dragon. Swedish explorers renamed it Drake, or dragon, Kill.

I can't blame the Jersey Devil for loving our coast, bastard waterfront that it is, shunted off by the state as he was by his mother. We had the power plant, Nick Agricola's oozing drums, everybody's waste. One family close by lost both their sons as teenagers to a rare form of leukemia; the sons swam in Toms River, by the Ciba-Geigy plant. Our weekly DDT truck left dead robins and redwinged blackbirds in the cattails.

A joke goes: what has the head of a ram, the body of a lion, the hooves of a goat, the wings of an eagle and is from New Jersey? The Jersey Devil or the average household pet in neighborhoods by the nuclear power plant.

And of course my grandfather loved our coast too, a misbegotten man, small and troll-like and gripped by silence. His affect would now be called depression but it seems to me something more. He did not sleep and sat up in the dark doing nothing. He died when I was eighteen and my memories of him spin around a sense of astonishing oldness, oldness as far back as I can remember, before he could have been that old: age dusty, flaking and folded in on itself in more folds than anyone could count, an oldness that seemed inhuman like a sibyl's.

When my grandfather was seven years old his father died. We know that his mother squandered her inheritance and then came to the United States from Barbados, my family's home since the 1600s; we don't know how long the squandering took or how old my grandfather was when he came. Clearly he was young enough to be dependent because when my greatgrandmother abandoned him he was taken in by a family named the Goslings, whom he met through a schoolfriend. After the death of his younger brother, Frederick—the fourteenth and last child—my grandfather took off for Canada and cooked in a logging camp. He became a Canadian citizen, then U.S.

My grandfather did not sail or swim or suntan—something no one from the tropics would ever do, knowing as they do that the sun is out to kill them every minute of the day. But he loved our bungalows and our coast and walking to the end of the street to watch our bay lift its curled palm at him from behind its wooden bulkhead. He liked the crabbers who chainsmoked as they picked mesh traps out of the water and baited them with fishheads. He liked to watch all of us traipse in and out of the house as he sat in the corner doing nothing—a man who liked to feed his solitude with movement. He had a way of sinking into his chair so his clothes bagged and wrinkled and he seemed to be a piece of empty fabric thrown there, waiting for something and watching.

Our bungalows and tiny beach stood on one side of an open round of water, an inlet within the inlet, that we called with no consciousness of sarcasm the yacht basin. Its "yachts" were my uncle Joe's small wooden sailboat and a bunch of bunged-up dinghies and outboarder crab boats. We had a wooden rowboat that took in slightly more water than you could bail out, so you had to time your rowing trips to get home before you sank.

Everything nautical in my family got handled by my uncle Joe. He came from a coalmining town in the mountains of western Pennsylvania, a town of Irish immigrants whose salaries went to the company store and who lived on nothing. During the Depression he and his family lived for a week or so on raisins; he could never again stand the sight of them, and if he saw one of us kids with so much as a raisin cookie he'd chase us out of the house.

His discipline consisted of chasing and not much else. He and my aunt slept in the Little Bungalow, with Mark in the next room, and lots of times in the yard we suddenly heard his bellowed

"Mark! MARK . . . "

Then two sets of feet pounded furiously around the cottage and Mark flew out into the yard, his father just behind him. When my uncle caught up with his son he picked him up and flipped him around in the air two or three times. That was it. That's what he did to all of us, Mark mostly, when he got mad. It wasn't at all a joke but getting chased by uncle Joe wasn't exactly scary either.

At age ten Joe had to go down into the mines to work, to make money for his family. At sixteen he ran away from home and joined the Merchant Marines and learned to sail. In my childhood, he worked in a sheetmetal shop.

I remember him, young, as handsome, choleric, roughly loving. He threw me higher up in the air than anyone else could and always had time for kids, especially the girls, since he had no daughter. On his boat, though, we did the scutwork like pumping bilge, and he expected us to act without question and obey orders.

"Get those damn brogans off!" he screamed if we got on board with hard shoes instead of sneakers.

My mother was given a great deal of her father. Like him she is small and still. She tends to pick a corner chair and sit with a book—a mystery or biography but never a novel—in too little light. She also works crossword puzzles for hours and hours. Like her father, she reveals when you talk to her that she's angry about a lot of things, welfare and taxes and county officials who want to test our well. Mostly she sits quietly and every once in a while asks a question like the name of Nabokov's lover of the juvenile, seven letters, ends with T.

It was the greatest puzzle of the first twenty years of my life whether my mother liked me or not. She gave no signs one way or another that I can remember. When I got on a bus to go nine hours away to college her eyes teared up and I figured that she did.

My brother and cousins and I spent a lot of time rowing around in our leaky rowboat, pitting ourselves against the water that started as a sweet massage on the toes and soon became an ankle wash and then brought the gunwale of the boat down level with the bay or river we rowed on. We had several old bleach bottles with the bottoms cut off for bailers but even two kids bailing furiously could only buy an hour or so of rowing time, and that done with a good amount of water in the boat. Our rowboat functioned as the inland sea equivalent of a shark cage, a barrier between the water we trusted our limbs to and the water outside that held crabs, sharptoothed fish like oyster crackers and, in the rivers, water moccasins, poisonous swimming snakes.

We rowed down Cedar Creek, actually a meandering little river, tannic colored and lined with Atlantic white cedars. Sometimes we rowed far enough up Cedar Creek to visit friends of my grandparents named the Needs. Our rowboat could not stay dry for this trip so we always ended up jumping out and pushing it the last way.

"You first!" Chris, Mark, Helen and I shouted at once.

Our friend Bobby Koller once jumped over the side with his feet in a bucket, Mark told him so many stories about the snakes.

Then the Needs, an old couple, gave us peanut butter sandwiches on china plates and we'd tip the boat over to empty it and row back.

My cousin Mark also had a sailboat that didn't sail, a twelve-footer called the *Redwing* that had been in the family forever. It had once been my mother's, a fact that astonished me—she seemed so passive and glued to her two activities, filling blank lines with words and drinking words off filled lines—that I couldn't picture her doing what you do with a boat. But apparently she sailed when young and somehow got the *Redwing*, a tub so unseaworthy she capsized pretty much every time you sailed her and, when capsized, couldn't be righted in any kind of a swell.

My family at the shore—my mother and my aunt Kathleen and my grandparents and whoever else—accepted, in a way that seemed philosophical if not exactly Buddhistic, that our sailboat didn't sail and our rowboat didn't row and that they were ours regardless and had to be given a daily chance to be what they were, whatever happened. Or something like that. We had a kind of communal acceptance of rowboats that gushed and sailboats that capsized and swimming water you'd contort yourself rather than step down into.

The family ran my uncle's sailboat, *Tara*, aground nearly every sail by tacking up too close to Island Beach, where the water level changed too fast to follow on a depth sounder. When we ran aground we children had to serve as ballast, hanging our bodies off the side of the boat with hands clutched to the rigging to pull the keel out of the muck. It could be practically impossible but still on our next sail we'd say, Let's go look at Island Beach, and whoever stood at the tiller would do it.

Though we wouldn't have admitted it we had, in our embracing of the unworkable, a Pine Barrens spirit. Pineys descend from a people who came by choice to the dragon's place, a region of boglands and difficult if not impossible soil, and made their homes. Most escaped devils more immediate—fallen kings, lost causes and the law. They've lived with and faithfully reported gutted chickens and dogs and sheep as well as those nightshrieks with their edge of hysterical irony. Of all the many attempts to capture or kill the Jersey Devil not one has come from a piney, though there've been decades when going out after dark in the Barrens would be proof of a disordered mind. This is a region of putting up and shutting up, where nothing is guaranteed: where pitch pines stop at five feet tall and are all the more terrible for that.

In fact we'd found our rowboat in the lagoon behind the bungalows, washed up after a violent storm. Kept it and used it but never fixed it. Our local dwellings were known for their scavenged materials: curved ship's timbers, corrugated cardboard, old sails. And their tendency to collapse back into pools of wreckage after squalls.

The Jersey Devil story has a natural climax, though it happened a hundred years ago and doesn't amplify the story, just introduces more of the human element. In one week of January 1909 the creature appeared to thousands of people. It appeared all over the Barrens but also broke out of the Barrens and terrorized nearby cities, causing the city of Camden to shut down. The Devil flew alongside trolley cars and fought the Collingswood Fire Department and got whupped by the broom of a Mrs. Sorbinski of Camden until it let go of her poodle.

Eventually it terrorized much of the Delaware Valley and held the headlines of every paper in the area, including all the Philadelphia papers, for the week and long thereafter. Newspaper sketch artists outdid themselves. Some drew the thing straight from a detailed description provided by a couple who observed it on their roof: the polyglot creature of ram and bat and dog. Others sketched fanciful flying gryphons or, for some reason, well-accoutred demons in tail-coats and breeches. The media made up nicknames for the Devil and speculated that Mother Leeds was a traitor and a witch and newspaper writers polished the skills that would shine in five years, when World War I broke out.

People woke up all week to the eerie screaming, cloven prints on their roofs and for one farmer, after the laughter, a field of strangely dead chickens, claws up and, for a change, not a mark on them.

Sunday of that week, January 23, 1909, the sightings stopped. Or they returned to the Barrens, which amounted to the same thing. Two men shipped a kangaroo in from Australia and painted it with purple stripes and pinned a tail on it and charged the public a quarter to see the Jersey Devil captured. A boy sat in the shadows of the kangaroo's cage and poked it with a sharp stick until it rushed in pain at the bars, so it would look fearsome.

As a result of this when my grandfather chose our shore land and began building in 1932 he chose land that lay under a stigma still. Even though the war had come the public remembered the Devil and its national headlines very well twenty years later. People remembered how the thing dressed, what meat it liked, its sassy posture in the news-paper sketch, paws on hips under a waistcoat and cloven feet shoulder-width apart. Its cry had become a commonplace. In fact the outbreak of the war hadn't eroded the Devil's press but enhanced it, since the creature's always been said to appear in places building for war, feeding off the evil. More outbreaks of sightings came before World War II, before Pearl Harbor and Vietnam and other conflicts.

In the 1930s, at the height of the Great Depression, the Jersey Devil was declared the state's Official Demon.

During the week of 1909, when the Devil finally broke out of the Pine Barrens, my grandfather was in one of the eclipsed phases of his life. I think he may have wandered around Canada that year, but I don't know. It seems odd to me that his four children don't know anymore about him, his doings over the years, but they don't seem to want to know.

Like the pineys, who would never organize posses or mobilize dogs and militias to hunt their Devil as outsiders did in 1909 (with no luck), we tolerated incursions into our space without grumbling or thinking much. People broke into our cottages and stayed for long periods whenever we weren't there; we found the evidence all over, grease in the frying pan, cans of Schlitz and Pepsi. It was ridiculously easy to break into the Big Bungalow. You just unlatched the screen of a back window and opened the window from the outside and climbed in. We broke into the houses as often as we used the key. One bedroom, the middle one, was for some reason equipped with a door that locked and windows that couldn't be opened from outside. It was the only safe place in the cottages and though my parents slept there when we went down the shore I got in the habit of dropping in to feel the catch of the doorlock and the soft bump—like stopping in a vertiginous fall—of containment.

———————

The adults in the family knew who broke into our house: someone who lived across the yacht basin.

"Oh, that's so-and-so," they'd say, and start cleaning up. "I wish he'd throw out his junk." They never spoke to so-and-so as far as I remember. So-and-so may have existed at some point in the universal order beyond being spoken to. Like the two middle-aged men who lived together in a shack, also across the yacht basin, who survived on crabs and berries and blowfish and seemed not to understand anyone but each other. They died in a murder-suicide, hounded to death by teenage boys who danced around their shack every night in sheets, hollering. Whenever the boys came and danced the two men yelled and sobbed in terror.

We had a beach party every year at our beach, little as a goodsized 1990s housing lot. The beach party involved mostly throwing Frisbees and eating raw clams and satisfying the yearly tradition of creating a mudman.

"Mudman! Mudman!" When it felt like time an orgiastic cry went up.

A man got picked, somebody older, half drunk, and he ran to the lagoon behind our bungalows and threw himself into a mosquito trench. Mud back there hangs viscous as potter's clay, greenishblack on the skin, so the mudman did not drip but emerged caked and almost dry, the slimeblack of seaweed, a fetish (our mudmen were always ample men, with pots and jowls, plenty of folds where the mud could crack and reveal the human lineaments). The mudman hurled himself back onto the beach at a dead run and raced in circles bellowing, not directing himself at the children, not at girls in bikinis or anyone in particular, but to the place itself. Then he jumped from the top of the stairs into the bay.

———

Once during a ratcheting blinding storm, maybe the edge of a hurricane, our backdoor pounded and Mark opened it to see a drenched old sailor in a macintosh whose mouth opened and closed, opened and closed—a black circle like the pupil of an eye dilating and closing around the shabby contents of our house, which he stared into and drank: the peeling cabbage-rose wallpaper and oval shadows of kerosene fire and brackish smoke. The thunder said and rain insinuated but this one defined place of utterance—the mouth—refused its function. Opening and closing.

Zero, the man said. Zero, zero, zero.

Or, Nothing nothing nothing.

Mark stood stuck in terror with his hand on the door. Finally a second sailor ran up and said their boat had wrecked and the man in the macintosh was a mute. We brought them in and fixed them coffee.

Of the mute man it seemed to me the magnetism of my grandfather's silence drew him. My grandfather was compact and nondescript, pale with that full and sulky lower lip. But he moved in a channel of quiet and where he sat the room hushed and leaned into him and grew nervous. He'd only talk about the corruption of politics and his experiences in World War I. He had the bullet in his neck and slept one night in a graveyard as shells rained around him; he'd used a corpse for cover. He got mad at my father for calling violent people animals. "Men are less than animals," he said. He had no other conclusions. He'd become this censer of silence, with an air of sucking the sound out of the human atmosphere by his contempt.

For all the bijouterie I've flashed about devils and mudmen and dead chickens it's actually that lock on the back bedroom, a keyless lock in a square box, a lock you punched down with a thumblatch, that's the

key, if I can use a pun, to this story. When I was ten and my grandfather tried to get me into bed with him I ran into that bedroom and
thumblatched the door, which is what I remember most, a heavy old
door painted the same denatured blue as our possessed table. And
because it locked I could stay in there until my father and brother
came back.

I told my brother a year later and he told me to forget it, no one
would believe us, a response I believe now was compassionate and
true.

Though in some ways that few minutes form the clearest memory
I have I've read so much about this kind of memory that I fear taint to
the image. I can unfold it with the clarity of a newsreel, with one blurry
spot, and maybe that's what worries me—the clear sharp lines of the
sketch artist, putting the Jersey Devil in his Edwardian topcoat.

My grandfather lay in the bottom cot of the bunkbed facing the
door, in the back bedroom. He lay on his side in a kind of crouch. One
hand clutched the covers up to his chin, a tense hand, veiling and full
of revelation.

"Come here," he said.

When I didn't move he repeated himself and threw the covers back.

Then I saw nude skin and my head blurred. Time became space
and swam past me physically, through and around. The altered space
ends when my hand touches the rough blue door and opens it and
closes it behind me and thumbs the latch. My parents' suitcase lurched
open on the floor: boxer shorts, Noxzema, a sixties one-piece swim-
suit with those oval cups plasticked in place so it looked like women
took their breasts off too. I sat on the edge of the bed and didn't move
until I heard the wiry spring of the backdoor and my father's voice, an
hour or so later.

————

I've read the opinions of biologists and zoologists who think the Jersey Devil's probably just a sandhill crane, a rare crane with a high piercing scream and a huge wingspan—eighty inches. That the crane doesn't eat flesh and can't fly with a hole in its middle are facts hard but not impossible to reconcile. A Professor Bralhopf believed it might be a prehistoric flying creature from the Jurassic, a pterodactyl or somesuch, that survived in an underground cavern. Like the coelacanth, a Cretaceous fish considered extinct and discovered swimming off the coast of Africa in 1938. It seems awfully human for a dinosaur, taunting the fire department, cavorting around a trolley car in Clementon, valuing its friend the headless sailor, giving up in the face of brave Mrs. Sorbinski and her broom. I suppose the greatest achievement of January 1909 was the collective certainty that the creature existed, that dispassionate experts who drew killers in the defendant's chair could draw the Devil. Until, of course, hundreds of people happily paid a quarter to see a purplepainted kangaroo.

Anyway, the story isn't over. Websites still post Jersey Devil sightings, often by concertgoers or travelers from Philadelphia to the Jersey shore who see it while driving the pale old highways. Same creature, with its scaly skin, "greedy, frightening grin" and wings. One report goes on about its stench, another Devil characteristic that goes back forever in reports: an "old-dead-clam-and-fish-head bay" smell, the writer says, weird as the creature appeared before him far inland, on an open field near Great Egg. One posting says that though the creature looked just like its descriptions, it also looked inexplicably like Julius Caesar.

Sitting in the Little Bungalow we used to hear strange screeches at night, one of the sounds of the area we got used to, or semi–used to, like the tramping; Mark sometimes told us we'd heard a banshee and because of that, one of us would die. Lately I've been wondering if one of us ever saw the Devil. I don't mean me exactly but some member of my family. No one of us would say if we did. We're pineys I believe now; we move along and cook and sleep on the shifting aquifer, and things like the Devil become just another initiation into silence, into the gritty stoicism of our place.

Chapter Nine

Double Helix

My mother and father are adenine and cytosine. My mother and father who shift from room to room all day like dollhouse figures are guanine and thymine. Their splitlevel has ornament shelves that hold knickknacks, tchotchkes, ceramic Siameses, a glass ball made of Mt. St. Helen's ash. Things that wink over the years because at least their foolishness doesn't age or change. My mother and father worry too much to leave these things for long. Twice a year I visit, with cytosine, thymine and guanine.

My greatgrandmother Berenda who motes with her fourteen children, two of whom died terribly, is adenine and thymine. My Bajan greatgrandfather no one knows and my Italian greatgrandfather and his pliant wife and my grandparents with their spirits are cytosine, guanine and adenine. I hold them in handcuffs or in a ballroom where they dance a pavane changing and rechanging partners and never sit or choose. They are not a corm from which I grow harmlessly. They're a field of graves rifled and open. When I miscarried five years ago I felt the breath of desperation on my face. Guanine, thymine, adenine, cytosine. The four bases of DNA.

When I was a teenager with a drug problem my parents liked to say, No one in the family has done that. No one has dropped out of high school. No Cassill has had these problems.

My manic-depression grew and sometimes I could feel my heart beating so hard and so fast it began to push my ribcage aside and emerge. I called out to my parents to tell them my heart was leaving.

No one in our family has ever had this, they'd say. We have good hearts.

Of course their denials about the family were lies though generally they believed them. Belief is so much a matter of desire and we're loaded with it: adenine, cytosine, guanine.

I remember planning my suicide at the age of eight or nine (Extra-Strength Excedrin, a bottle) and I remember the reverse: waking up with what I called my "good stomachache" and watching the world bloom out of my midsection. My red medical manual says *Manic-depression or bipolar disorder typically arises during the mid-twenties* so I'm not sure what it is before. To me it's been the same. I don't remember ever not having wild mood swings and I had a series of names for myself to correspond with the personalities: Sue, Susie, Susanna, Susanne.

I could be normal or too harrowed to raise a finger or think I saw the future as if I were looking at a television set. Sometimes I woke up and found myself full of ground glass. I believed I could move things with my mind.

Who held whom by the hand? Certainly my greatgrandmother was manic-depressive or at least manic, and her daughter Rennie and probably other of her children. My cousin Mark is and I am and my grandfather had something wrong with him, God knows what. We come from a bipolar island, Barbados, half Atlantic and half Caribbean, half delicate white sand beaches and half deadly cliffs and surf.

It gets clearer and clearer that genes don't act alone, or disease rates wouldn't fluctuate the way they do: one out of seven women facing breast cancer and one out of five couples infertile at the end of the twentieth century. Genes create tendencies the environment can activate, as doses of radiation and toxic chemicals alter body and brain chemistry and also attack the chromosomes, helping recessive traits come forward. Genes and the environment can work separately or, most likely in a case like mine, together. When they and my mother and father mated, DNA danced wildly like a party at a lunatic asylum. Thymine, guanine.

Sometimes I think I'm really sick.
All of a sudden tears were running down my cheeks & I was hitting myself really hard with a hairbrush. (8/7/72, age 15)

My parents gave themselves away when they said this never happened before. They taught me this had a thisness, this had a name.

As soon as I learned I could change the interior of my mind, rearrange neurotransmitters like GABA and serotonin and dopamine myself with easily gotten things, I did as much as possible, starting when I turned thirteen. Another thing people in the family didn't do, my parents said in their faithful reports, mapping my latitude and longitude. This assertion as far as I can tell was true though we have had drunks and my grandmother had her opium cigarette, that pearled her existence for a while. I dropped out of high school. That had been done in spite of my parents' denials.

> Dear Diary,
> Hi again, well I'm tripping again & did a few downs.
> Sunday night I did junk acid downs smoke & liquor.   (1/23/72, age 16)

I can't help but admire a little the impulse behind drug use: the radical restructuring of a self, the almost-spiritual transference of all sense of reality to a place of otherness, a place that cannot be seen. Being medicated is passive. Someone pours into your mouth what will make you think the way they think.

It was the 1970s. The nation had been learning to lie, learning from television. For years we'd been secretly bombing the country of Cambodia. Our GIs came back from Vietnam, many sick from a herbicide called Agent Orange, used to waste Vietnamese jungles. Our Agent Orange was contaminated with dioxins, a fact denied for a long time, then confirmed.

Lying had become a ritual ceremonial act, one that's since become deeply embedded: every four years a man's face floats up in the ghost space of television, says things he doesn't mean and we do not believe, and we vote for him and spend the next four years watching those few months of promises unravel. As if we need that: a buildup and a jilting ("Read my lips!" "A swift end to the war."). As if we were bored.

But in the 1970s of Vietnam and Watergate the ritual was new and dramatic: John Mitchell saying the President knew nothing, Gordon Liddy barbecuing his palm in a candle. Nixon declaring his prior statements "inoperative"; Haldeman on tape: "You can say you've forgotten too, can't you." The subpoenaed tape of White House conversations with eighteen minutes missing—"When I reached for the phone I must have hit the pedal," blushed Rose Mary Woods, the secretary, and demonstrated her famous "stretch" for *Life* magazine photographers.

"Never Trust Anyone Over Thirty," was a slogan.

That feeling led to the creation of a culture that as far as I know has never existed before—a culture of children, legal dependents, making their own rules and living in their own world, lying too. This culture found in Richard Nixon and Vietnam its focus—Richard Nixon of Operation Intercept, who choked off marijuana from Mexico in 1969 and led millions of American teenagers to move on to hallucinogens. Who appeared on television in floury makeup but whose charcoal jowls and skislope nose could not be masked. He appeared like a Dorian Gray portrait of those whose representative and embodiment he was, a reason to fool those whose ruler was not just a supreme liar but such a bad one—a man who could not even fool television.

Now I pass a bumpersticker on my way to and from work everyday. It's a nineties slogan: *SAVE THE PLANET. KILL YOURSELF.*

We used to think, for no obvious reason, we were the answer.

Aug. 7, 1972
Dear Diary,
Hi! tonight me & Alice split a downer & smoked pot & got pretty fucked up. Tomorrow night, tho, we'll be really flying. My parents are going out & we're buying some soapers. So me & Al will be doing the soapers, drinking beer, and smoking pot all night.
This afternoon I hitched to Elizabeth with Alice. I hocked some makeup & bought 4 packs of rolling papers, 1 really dynamite pack of cinnamon flavored ones.

To the extent that we could deceive adults we wanted to, using the abrasive of little lies to scour away the great ones unfolding before us.

And in a sense this is all excuses—lies, in other words.

Soapers was my misspelling of the street name *sopor*, a barbiturate.

What bothered my husband when he read my diaries, he said, was the question of what my parents were doing all this time. I stayed out all night or went into nods on the couch or puked my way to my bed. The answer is they were doing what they did, going to work, worrying about when they could afford a bigger house farther out in the suburbs, with a second bathroom.

Every day they said to me, "What are you doing?"

I said, "Nothing."

"Are you on drugs?" my father asked me once in a while.

I told him, "No."

Whatever I said they accepted, sadly. There was precedent for this.

My friend Alice chewed gum and wore hotpants with clogs or go-go boots and had enviably straight dirty blond hair. All my girlfriends dressed like her, and if they didn't have straight hair they ironed their hair or wet it and slept with it rolled around orange juice cans to straighten it. At fifteen I had a cool boyfriend too. Kenny: twenty-two, a dealer, who looked a lot like Peter Fonda in *Easy Rider* and had an apartment full of dope and guns. Our best friend Jimmy worked as a narcotics cop and dealt on the side with what he busted. Dealers' money comes in erratically and profits go to merchandise so when Kenny needed extra cash he roofed. He took a lot of pride in his roofing and never missed a chance to describe himself as a roofer. It strikes me as funny now how everyone I knew, no matter how far they lived outside the law, loved placing themselves somehow inside the capitalist foodchain.

We talked like we worked for Mattel. We used the word "product" incessantly.

The Hell's Angels, those blackslicked emptiers of bars, keep a PR company on retainer and have a president, vice president and local committees.

———

I wrote on a notebook in 1972

What happens if you die when you're tripping—do you ever crash?

(This was our idea of deep.)

Middle of the afternoon, 1972. Nixon has his party's blessing to run for President again. He stands on the platform at the Republican Convention in a snowstorm of balloons, red, white and blue. The balloons drop from a secret place in the ceiling and dozens bump against his body, pausing in the crooks of his arms and shoulders. Bright, simple, pleasing and light, like everybody's ideas about the future levitating together in the air.

When we come across this on television—the group of kids I'm with, a bright and simple group—we watch for a second and keep going.

Kenny says, "What if the people on TV can see us? I mean, really see us? What if they just sit there, like, pretending they can't."

What they'd see: five kids ranging in age from fifteen (me) to twenty-five (Rick Marino), fullface, lips open and shiny—five trout with the electronic hook in the mouth. Sprawled on ratty furniture, jeans, clogs, leather boots.

We find the *Hollywood Squares,* something we can relate to. The moderator asks Paul Lynde if he thinks people should live together before marriage. Paul Lynde hesitates, quips, "Would you buy an apartment before you knew whether the furniture would fit?"

"Aw," says Rick, "why buy the fucking apartment anyway."

"Do they have backs on that thing?" says Quail (his name is really Pasquale) of the grid where the Hollywood celebrities sit. "Or could they, like, push their chairs back and fall off."

Kenny says, "Do you think they get paid more than five hundred a day to do that? Do people like that pay taxes?"

Rick says, with his wise man air, "Nah, they pay lawyers."

After a while there's just two-phrase bursts of conversation: *Louder it.*

Why cuz?

It's afternoon. Two tarry glass bongs on the scarred coffee table. The air sweet with the smell of hashish cooked down to pure THC. Three lava lamps are squirting their chemical ovals back and forth, like Nixon's balloons. We're in Kenny's apartment in Kenilworth, in a kind of housing project; out the window we see tiers of identical peeling apartments. The guys have just shot up, which they do in the bathroom, like all the guys I know do if a woman's around—even one who shoots up herself—out of a weird sense of chivalry.

We're all messed up and full of questions, like the one about whether each cell in our body could be its own solar system.

A knock at the door. Kenny peeks out over the windowsill and whisper-shrieks. *Cop.* We're all movement. In a second the toilet's clogged: a rusty old basin, none too clean, into which Baggies are emptied. The oval of water crusted with hard darkgreen lumps, a thick dusting of powder, islands of red pills, dried weed. Flush flush. Kenny runs to get the door.

He comes back embarrassed.

"He just wanted to sell us tickets or something."

We settle back in front of the TV. Kenny's in no shape to mourn his losses yet.

Kenny had product. He sold everything he could when he could: grass, heroin, coke, acid, PCP, exotics like peyote buttons, and he had a lot of different sources. One was Jimmy the narc and one was our friend Debbie's mother Mrs. Player, who also dealt for a living and gave Debbie's ten-year-old sister a few hits of windowpane acid for Christmas one year, wrapped up with a ribbon in a cottoned jeweler's box.

I saw Carol a few days ago, she's doing pretty good. Anne Licata's busted, and has six months' probation. (8/31/72)

I wrote dispassionately, dutifully, like a reporter. I think about that woman inhabiting the body of the woman who now works as a college professor, who plants bulbs and grades papers and brings stray spaniels home, to live out their lives scuffing in the soil.

When I was fourteen or fifteen dozens of my friends got raided at a party I decided at the last minute not to go to. I sat on a curb in Elizabeth and cried over the newspaper where I read the story and saw the list of their names. A middle-aged woman in curlers came over and asked if she could help. I blurted out no and ran, afraid she'd call the cops out of a misguided compassion. We treated straight people like bears, who, friendly or not, could crush the life out of you if you happened to come in their sight.

I feel like shit—Mike didn't call tonite—
I found out today that Kevin Conway, my ex-boyfriend, is in jail for attempted murder. He somehow severed ~~por~~ poor John-John's hand while trying to stab him. It shocked the hell out of me because a few weeks ago Kevin asked me back. I kept thinking 'it could have been me, it could have been me, it could have been me.'
I wasn't scared or anything, just fascinated. (8/3/72, age 15)

I wept bitterly when boys I liked didn't call, or, after I hooked up with Kenny, if we argued or he flirted with someone else. I don't remember any thought over the stump where a boy's hand had been, or for another friend institutionalized after a bad acid trip, or for all the second-rate dealers beaten out of their dope so it could be sold by a cop. Kenny came home to the apartment one day with a harpoon gun, a monstrous thing. I played with it and pressed the tip into my palm where without pressure it raised a neat virgule of blood: beautiful. I helped him hang it within arm's reach over the bed.

I woke more than once from a heroin nod to find a cigarette burning into the thin skin of my palm. I remember looking at the skin flame as if it were done to amuse me, a theatrical trick, story of saint and stigmata.

Such a removed quality to our looking.

It was a kind of lying, this tunnel vision, this look at just a tiny eyehole of our violent and homemade world.

One day Jimmy's wife Neesie settled their baby into the car when holes grew in the windshield, pop pop pop. These spread out fissures that reached for the other holes like neurons connecting in the brain. Somehow the shooter, also in a car, missed them. Jimmy narked people out, and while dealers considered him a dealer cops considered him undercover. He made money on both ends and treated the force as the ultimate scam. This was pretty common. Among our set only Kenny and I had his real identity but I guess someone else suspected; the shooter targeted Neesie because she and Jimmy had the same Afro and she looked like him from the back.

I remember this shooting clearly though I don't seem to have considered it worth writing about.

Drugs fall through many levels of packaging and repackaging, like apples or shoes or Barbies. At some point the product's pure but the market's job is adding more and more layers of impurity. We were the seven material heavens spirits fall through to pad out with mortal flesh.

What we bought—say a bag of coke—came with a purity percentage.

"It's 97," the seller would say, which was of course a lie.

Then whatever the percentage was we cut the drug further and sat around Kenny's wooden kitchen table, me and him and some friends who helped out in the business, spooning out smaller amounts to fill up smaller Baggies.

Some things like speed we stuffed into gelcaps we got by buying vitamin pills at pharmacies and fluffing out the vitamin powder. Kenny cooked up concentrated THC from hashish and we rolled it into sticky pellets we shoved into caps. When you do packaging inevitably you absorb lots of drug through your skin so before you know it you're flying—it's called *making contact.* Contact highs can be wicked because you can't judge your exposure: sometimes I'd look up to see someone at the table frozen, struck into oblivion, openmouthed and raw.

Sometimes I'd look at myself and see the cap in my hand half melted and realize I hadn't moved in a long, long time.

Like the priests called to bedsides during the plague, suddenly unmoving, struck dead while hearing the confessions of the sick.

My family was oddly nice to me then. I created blindnesses. They were compassionate. They respected this project. They agreed not to notice me when I passed out on sofas at night, unable to lurch to my bed: the shape so like my grandfather's insomniac shape. I was Proteus. I spoke many languages, some incoherent. In a sense I was who I was meant to be.

We swallowed these selves, with their mutable bodies and strange, corner-of-the-eye vision. We communed and we changed. The small clarity of a hit of windowpane, a Quaalude's stubby, soporific wafer: the christic body. A spoon blistering with lazy bolls of cooking heroin: the tarry blood. As a community of believers we made our eschaton, an infinity of mindless arousal, swallowed it, and intermittently achieved it. Our substance altered.

———

I met a man at a party in Elizabeth. An older man. He asked for my number and I gave it to him.

The first time he called me he said, "I'll get you all the downs you want. Free."

He talked quickly, like a carnival barker.

"I'd like to buy you a nice dress. Purple. Pretty. A sizzler. A pair of hotpants."

After a few calls he told me he had girls who worked for him who had sex with people, and made money, and had all the things they wanted.

"Get some extra cash, a little money in your pocket. Buy yourself some nice things," he said. "A dress, you know, like a comb."

When I remember him I wonder why the comb. He called me a lot, for months, and always mentioned it. Smart, implying a small reward meant a small sacrifice. Or maybe I seemed so young he figured a comb would appeal to me as much as anything else. I can see now how good a prospect I must have been: young but mature-looking, well-developed, reasonably pretty, heavily enough into drugs to be controlled.

I said no after thinking about it for a while. My boyfriends kept me well supplied with drugs, and I've always been a lazy person: I don't work for what I don't need. No other reason existed. My body was lost to me anyway. I pummeled away at it myself, shocking and stuporing the central nervous system, faking out the brain's neurochemical messengers like someone teasing a bunch of stupid but overeager dogs. Was it ever mine? My world had made a new air for me to breathe and a new water for me to drink. I had growths in me that did not belong, thoughts in my head that didn't seem in any way to be mine; I was foreign, infiltrate. To possess my own body, I had to replace it with whatever matter I could choose. It wasn't the flesh I had but the flesh I ate, the flesh I aspired to.

Double Helix

Memory is a form of lying. Autobiography is a literary form devoted to the ceremonial lie. A taxidermy. A pretense that the form of what's dead can be preserved, made to lash and snarl still. When I found my diaries a decade ago I found chunks of the past preserved, viewed from the distance of a few hours' worth of memory rather than fifteen years' worth. Not only were my memories wrong, I found, but my memories of how I remember were wrong. I considered myself an exaggerator, someone who would embellish, turn a little cut into a severed hand. In fact, I minimized my old life to myself, trying desperately in memory to normalize. I recalled using heroin a handful of times, though I had used it regularly, daily, for more than a year.

> I gotta quit doing *heroin* & *LSD* but I can't they're my 2 favorite hi's.
> (1/13/73, age 16)

My self-story was that I couldn't use needles because of my recessed veins (those Radford veins, guanine and thymine) but after an overdose I wrote

> I have to wait til I can screw up my courage again enough to OD but good. I'm gonna shoot it this time—that's easier. (1/23/73)

Did I shoot up? How many times? I don't have the heavy bloating on my arms that means years of regular use. I do have some pinpoint scarring but found these diaries after years of weekly blood tests for lithium, depakote, liver function, thyroid function, so the scarring could mean nothing at all.

> Jan. 13, 1973
> Dear Whatever the fuck u are,
> Hi! I haven't written anything in a long time but I wanted to tonite cause I'm tripping & I want to see if I can. I did a hit of 4barrel blotter smoked a little drank a little got some pot why not. No I'm being silly I can write straight. Me & Joanne went tripping tonit—first to a party at Dougie

Banfield's, then to a movie, SRO, split for Burger King (hitched), badassed the cops, talked to our friends, got a ride to my house, J. left, here I am. It's 1:30 & I am tripping my balls off. All the woodwork looks so pretty, like its moving. Everything looks pretty. I love LSD—I've tripped 15 times since Christmas. New Year's Eve I did 2 hits of purple haze & quite a bite of heroin & smoked a lot & drank. I was rather ripped. I *love* heroin & LSD together plus pot & downs & a little beer—its my favorite hi. What a rush—trying to write when I'm tripping. I saw Greg tonite—he's pissed cause he wanted me to hang all over him. Dougie's been drinking himself to death lately—he likes me. I think I'm gon commit ~~so~~ suicide cause whats the use of living if you're always plastered & even then you're not happy? I'm a half-way junkie now—where will I be in a couple years?

I gotta quit doing *heroin & LSD* but I can't they're my 2 favorite hi's. I wish I had a cool steady boyfriend. Woo, I can't believe I can write—I'm tripping so heavy & feeling very weird & hi. Tonit at the King everything was red & blue esp. the woodwork. I was cracking up over the pig. I'm sick—I know only a few people who could stand to do as much drugs as I can all at once—one's Kevin Conway—look how he ended up.

This is a rush—I see beautiful designs flowing from the pen. Gotta go beddy bye
  Susanne
  Acid Queen

Under the writing is a half-page of empty space filled with my drawings: a fanged ghost, two wide lidless eyes (better sketched than anything I could do now). Alice Cooper lyrics. *Bodies need rest, sleep, an easy sleep.*

This is the story of a body. In the twenty-six years since I wrote this my ten trillion cells have replaced themselves three times, except the doled-out brain cells, which don't replenish. In this period my thyroid cells, many of them, became something other than thyroid cells; their DNA altered, they lost their purpose and began filling up my neck.

The ovaries I had then are gone. I've grown lesions on my liver. My uterine lining has moved out and now resides in the pelvis. I take pills that stream into the brain the GABA and serotonin that isn't naturally there. The DDT that tucked into my cells then has dissipated, though not its effects. I am rarely near Oyster Creek and no longer (probably) made of tritiated water. Though there's no way to end the generations of poisoning: the years my landscape poisoned me, the years that, to compensate, maybe, I poisoned myself.

I weighed nothing then, barely a hundred pounds on a 5'6" body. Now I displace one-third more air. I could not write that way if I tried. I could not draw that way if I tried.

I cannot stuff and pose this girl. I do not know her.

I kicked drugs at seventeen, years out of school, years of drugs behind me. A different person from the one I had been four years before, not in my ten trillion cells but in the brain—functionally, in the way it worked, in the memories it housed. Cleaning up wasn't anything I planned to do. I took a big overdose of methadone and got sick—puking, inhumanly nauseated—for a week. I didn't mean to take it; my boyfriend Kenny dosed me, slipping the liquid methadone into an orange soda.

That sickness was the kind where you're so sick your body wants to throw up even what's not in it, where if you could you'd will your liver, kidneys, brain, heart, chromosomes to follow the brute peristaltic motion out. Even the color orange sent me off gagging for a long time, and I've never had an orange soda again. Whatever I went through of withdrawal must have folded into the general sickness of that week. Finally though I saw what lay in front of me. Toilet, stomach contents, nauseous orange. There was my face, in that mirror. Pale, yellowish, heaving its substance out. It was an epiphany, that what I was doing I couldn't keep doing.

About a week after I cleaned up I experienced an incredible peace, as if I had swallowed a hymn and it lay crooning softly in my gut. It was greater even than heroin. And though the feeling hasn't come back, it gave me something new and impossible to reach for.

Chapter Ten

Midway House

At fifteen, after several overdoses, I spent time in a mental institution, on a ward for kids. It was located in the middle of nowhere in south Jersey, somewhere flat and scrubby, full of the nonsense noise of crickets. Most of the kids had some version of a drug problem, though the place offered no drug treatment. It offered almost no treatment of any kind, and was pretty much just a warehouse, taking our parents' health insurance and feeding off their desperation, allowing us to recreate our outside lives within that long low building and rigid envelope of scheduled hours.

We'd have, say, an exercise hour where we'd squat in the corner and talk, and a group therapy hour where we'd get herded into a room and squat in the corner and talk. Then TV for an hour; we'd semi-circle around the set and talk some more.

We spent just a few minutes a week with a therapist unless you count occupational therapy, which consisted mostly of games like *Monopoly* and Chinese checkers. I've never met a drug user who wasn't phenomenal at board games; we could play for hours, and were perfectly happy.

I hung out with two girls my age, Carol and Yvonne, and my roommate, Suzanne, who was nineteen. Carol had ropy ragged hair and ropy ragged arms; she self-mutilated with glass and razors. Yvonne, a truckdriver's daughter, looked like a pixilated Barbie doll and shot heroin. She'd tried to kill herself by shooting an overdose, then swallowing a pile of Seconals and chasing them with vodka and bleach. Like most serious shooters, as soon as she met me she appraised my arms and twisted them around, saying *Man* to their sunken whispers of blue.

Suzanne was different, a straight-A student at Princeton, a self-described Goody Two-Shoes who'd tried marijuana all of once. She called me her mirror image, the Baddy Baddy to her Goody Goody. Suzanne had tried to kill herself, legally, with sleeping pills. She told me right away she didn't mean to.

"I was tired," she said. "I needed to rest, I think I needed some attention.

"It was just a cry for help," she said, picking up a phrase the staff always used on would-be suicides, provocatively sometimes: *If you really wanted to do it you would do it.*

What I remember, in improbable color, was her body. When she undressed it slipped out from her baggy clothes, joined her plain scrubbed collegegirl face, a Rembrandt in a Quaker setting: a body beyond pornography, large rounded breasts with beautiful sunset nipples, a scooped waist and endless contoured legs. It was breathtaking. I lay on my side on my cot and watched her.

One night when we were lying in bed I asked her, "What do you think happens after you die?"

She said, "Nothing. Basically I think they throw you in the ground and you rot."

That seemed unlikely to me. I wavered a lot but always believed in something, reincarnation or heaven or just becoming a thinking blade of grass. Suzanne said she'd thought about it and she was sure: nothing. I couldn't believe anyone who felt that way would try killing themselves, even someone who didn't mean it, because with dying you could never tell.

We had plenty of drugs on the ward. Visitors brought them, and we figured out how to steal stuff from the doctor's rooms and nurses' stations, snatching at pharmaceutical samples and amber vials whenever backs were turned. What we could find we swallowed. Sometimes nothing happened and sometimes we'd go off into places we couldn't remember. The psychiatrist who ran the ward, Dr. Weber, and his staff lived in a state of fury at the patients' bold defiances, the pill popping and running away. They used what they had at hand for punishment.

Small infractions or failure to act responsive enough in therapy got ECT, electrical shock given to bring on convulsions. For more serious things like getting caught high they'd keep you awake and pump your stomach; for the worst stuff they kept you awake for electroshock. Normally for ECT after you're strapped in and the plastic tongue protector's jammed in your mouth and a nurse has smeared the jellied volt conductor on your temples a needle slides into your arm and puts you to sleep. But sometimes the staff denied anesthetic and just strapped the delinquent down and held her. I got plenty of electroshock but never pushed them far enough to get beyond threats of no anesthesia. Others did and said it felt like sticking your fingers into a hundred light sockets at once. Your body flopping like a trout on an emptied creek.

The patients had a song they sang when the electroshock cart went down the halls, to the tune of "The worms crawl in."

If you should see the buzzbox go by
Remember that when you get high
They hold you down with a leather strap
And buzz your brain out zap zap zap

Nixon hadn't won reelection yet—this was the spring of 1972—but his opponent George McGovern's campaign would fall apart soon, when McGovern's running mate, Tom Eagleton, admitted that years before he'd received shock treatment for depression. When the news broke McGovern pledged Eagleton "1000% support," then dropped him from his ticket.

Once I stole a bottle of pills and took most of it and ran away. We all ran away from time to time, when the staff forgot to lock the doors. The local cops knew a lot of the inmates by sight. I begged money on the street. I wanted to go somewhere but I don't know where: I couldn't think really. I went into a total blackout, a twilight place, and when I came back to myself I stood inside a Catholic church.

What I remember about that is the sense of having arrived somewhere—not my usual somewhere of a place to leave or to blur. A rightness: the glasscolored emptiness that waited, seemed to have waited for a long time, for my scarred body to disturb it. As if this dusty pastelled darkness needed a flaw, a life this helpless and purposeless and vague. To mirror its own purposeful formlessness.

A night nurse picked me up, an older woman named Mildred,

small and dark and wry. She had stopped in to light a candle or something and found me by accident. She drove me back to the hospital. I was crying at what Dr. Weber would do.

"Someday," she said, "you'll face a greater master than him or anyone." I didn't know what she was talking about.

"I took her out for the afternoon," she said a little too loudly at the front entrance, and clutched my arm. They believed her.

Suzanne and Yvonne were released before I was, Carol after. I didn't stay in touch with Carol.

> Yvonne called me up today. She might come up & stay with us Thursday-Sunday. I hope she can cause she's a cool person. I'm saving some downs & smoke for her if she comes.

Yvonne and I stayed friends for a while after Midway House. Close to a year later I called her and she told me she'd gone straight. She realized, she said, that her parents really loved her. She wanted her life back. All I could recall of her parents is that her mother had had a nose job, and Yvonne used to taunt her about it—say her nose was getting fat again.

> She's going to try & bring me some ups, & we're going to have a fucked up weekend. (8/15/72)

We lost touch. I had no room in my life for her then.

Suzanne's family acted strange when I called her, didn't want to talk to me. Her mother and father vaguely promised to pass on messages. Finally her mother told me Suzanne died in a car crash, slamming into a cliff a little while after her release. I never learned anything else: the details of what happened, whether it was really an accident.

When I tried to mourn Suzanne in a specific way my mind kept drifting to that body, mixed with the torn steel of a car and then buried. Rotting, if she was right and I was wrong.

Chapter Eleven

Radium Girls

I have an 1860s phrenologist's chart. It faces me and my computer, a feud between the smug knowing of two centuries. It maps the brain, or its bulges, with categories like "time" and "sublimity." Phrenologists read character by charting particular spots on the head. I don't know the technique—whether having a large region of sublimity tells if you aspire to become sublime, recognize and love the sublime or simply are sublime. And time? How much you have. Or how far it will seem to go.

When the X-ray was invented, in 1896, doctors tried to find the soul with it, scanning the cranium, the chest cavity, even the hands and feet.

Finding just bone after all, white staff of the soft tissue. And because science found the X-ray—radiation used to penetrate flesh—they found, eventually, atomic splitting and fission and the radioactive heat of nuclear power plants, and the bombs exploded in Hiroshima and Nagasaki. And maybe in the final analysis the rays did what they tried to do at the beginning—exposed the soul by melting the rest away.

Here's a fable.

It happened in Orange, New Jersey, during the first world war: a group of women, their hair, faces, arms, necks luminescent (the back of one, beautifully undraped like a Renaissance woman, glowing to the waist). Patches of light on the thighs, on the swell of the calf. Bits of the head, where the hair fell out—at sublimity? time? the node of benevolence?—lighted as the moon. Like stained glass.

The newspapers called them the Radium Girls.

They sat in the courtroom, toothless balding women.

Shortly after the discovery of the X-ray Marie and Pierre Curie isolated radium from pitchblende and watched it glow in the dark. Then came uses for it: the Radium Girls worked in a factory in Orange, New Jersey, near Elizabeth, where they painted watch and clock dials with radium paint, to make them glow in the dark with an uncanny greenish phosphorescence. They used brushes made of hair and mixed their paint from water, radium powder and some kind of glue. Every few minutes the brush ends splayed out and the women were told to point the ends with their lips. (*It didn't have any taste, and I didn't know it was harmful.*) The Radium Girls painted their nails sometimes with radium paint, playfully, and their teeth, to surprise their boyfriends with a lucid smile in the dark.

The most famous Radium Girl—Grace—blew her nose after working in the factory a while and found the handkerchief alive in the night, lit, spectral.

They became a trinity, the Radium Girls: their souls, their bodies, and the ghosts their bodies gave off.

Grace's last name was *Fryer*.

In another room of the factory U.S. Radium scientists (male) handled radium with lead screens, gloves and tongs. U.S. Radium had files of information on the poisonous effects of radium. The Radium Girls function like girls in Greek myth, set up for a metamorphosis involving beauty, death and light. A true story but a fable because it involves a brilliant transformation.

I live with the Radium Girls. I watch them in the courtroom, dying, glowing. I talk to them. I see their endless physicals, the reports of luminous patches here and here and here: I want to tell them about my endless physicals, the dark spots that turn up that are never supposed to exist. Maybe with their ethereal knowledge they could point to the jar of radium paint in my life, the brush smeared on my lips. I want my cousins and me to line up and be the Radium Girls, glowing lightly in the womb, the neck and in the brain.

"If we could hook you up to a PET scan, off meds, you'd light up. Your brain would," my doctor says. I love her. She looks a little like my Midway House roommate Suzanne, with long straight dark hair, seventies hair.

She says this with deep satisfaction, like she's Tom Edison and hopes to work into the night by the light of my brain. I've seen PET scans: mine would show deep blues and greens and a greenish-whitish glowing patch in the center, in the amygdala (Latin, the *almond*), the center of excitation. The amygdala lies near the frontal lobe, somewhere between the self-perfecting parts and the animal parts on my phrenologist's chart. Maybe closest to what he calls *ideality*.

This doctor first put me on depakote: like Lourdes after years of ineffective drugs. Depakote was experimental for manic-depressives then. I had lived with this condition much of my life, and for a long time the only drug widely prescribed for it was lithium. Lithium didn't work for me. It made me fat, gave me scarring acne, and I cycled anyway. The doctor who'd put me on lithium—a stooped gangly man with a scruffy horseshoe of hair—kept prescribing supplements until I took five or six different drugs—sleeping pills, antinausea drugs, tranquilizers and other stuff—with drugs to counteract the side effects of other drugs.

My lithium doctor killed himself with a gun. I found out when I went to get a prescription refilled.

The pharmacist, a woman with a nasal voice, blurted out, "I can't refill this. The doctor has expired."

I thought she meant *prescription.*

"No, doctor," she said, then, "Look, call his office."

Bruce called. The nurse used the same verb—*expired*—in a flat voice. An expired doctor. No one could step out from behind that huge irony. My doctor's wife, I found out later, killed herself too, with pills. I mourned them. He had been a kind man.

I noticed my doctors always had a drug of choice, something they believed in absolutely (proving they too have their gods). I had a haldol doctor, a pudgy man, suave and chilly.

"I have this drug I've found is very useful with my patients. It's called haldol. Sometimes it's not useful right away but when I give them more I find that it is useful."

Haldol creates a blank mind and a body stung with involuntary motor responses: instead of thinking, I kicked my legs and twitched my fingers. I told these doctors their regimens were not working. I hated being the visionary bearing the burden of their faiths.

———

Depakote and a similar drug, carbemazepine, are newer treatments for manic-depression or, to use the current term, bipolar disorder. Both are anticonvulsants; seizure drugs used to treat epilepsy that doctors noticed also worked on rapid-cycling manic-depressives— those who swing, like me, between depression and mania more than two or three times a year. Rapid cyclers show epileptiform activity on brain wave tests, the spikes and rapid firing that indicate overexcitement of the electrical circuits. Mania is like a little seizure, expressed somehow in mental thrashing.

One day I arrive for an appointment with my good doctor. I come to speak to her, to her long hair, and find her unpacking a box, lifting out something that looks like a Strawberry Shortcake cookie jar.

"Former patient," she says wryly. "They stay in touch and send stuff. They start to think of me as Mom."

I feel sheepish. I think of her as Mom, though she's my age. She's bipolar like me, a fact she tells some patients and not others. Her brain like mine would catch fire and glow in the magnetic resonance chamber, with a moonish glow in the center. Her name is even Mary like my mother's: Mary of the Moon.

When I was a child I was diagnosed with petit mal, a mild seizure disorder that's generally not treated. It consisted of trance or fugue states lasting a few minutes. Almost out-of-body time. Because the disorder consists of nothingness I can only remember the fugues if they happened in a memorable frame. Once I stepped before a car, that yanked to a halt in front of me. Once I sat in front of the grocery store in Bayville with a Coke can in my hands. I snapped to as a middle-aged woman tried to stuff dollar bills in it. When my eyes flicked up to her she flinched and stepped backward to her car.

"I thought she was blind," she mumbled to her daughter. "I thought she was blind."

A lot of the Radium Girls licked and dabbed and luminesced for the war effort. They painted watch and control dials for the soldiers, so they'd be able to see. We went back to the world of chemicals in the second world war, when our chemists bent masked and gloved over beakers and microscopes creating biological weapons. The science of organic chemistry took off then, in the course of learning to attack the human body—to kill its cells, rewire its brain, jelly its limbs and muscles. Its basis was the restructuring of the carbon atom, the building block of life, into new and insidious molecules that could penetrate and alter the basic functioning of the body. Many biological weapons were tested on insects. After the war, with stores of chemicals left over, it seemed reasonable to use them, somewhat diluted, to kill the bugs they'd killed with twitching efficiency in the labs.

The power of organic chemicals to alter basic substances made them ideal for industrial use—as solvents, catalysts, coolants, the bases for more industrial chemicals. We began to use classes of chemicals like the organophosphates—little changed from their original form as World War II's nerve gases—on our food crops and grazing grasses and in our factories, where they mixed into the sludges we sluiced out onto the land. Organophosphates work industrially and as pesticides, and they do kill people pretty frequently, mostly factory workers and farmers who spill or inhale them. Finnish suicides like to eat parathion. Americans put them on their lawns and gardens, under names like malathion, diazinon, fenthion.

Because we had planes left over from World War II and its bombing campaigns we began to use them to dust and drop pesticides from the air, at times spraying whole quadrants of the United States to bombard bugs like gypsy moths (in New York and New England) and fire ants (in the South), in a drive for what the government called *final eradication.*

Many chemicals attack the nervous system and the brain. They cause seizures, sometimes lasting epilepsy, wild emotional changes. Organophosphates do this, even in bees: poisoned bees fight and frantically clean themselves, like humans with obsessive-compulsive disorder, in the twenty minutes or so before they die. Radiation can have the same effect, by attacking the structure and functioning of the neurons. Chemicals and radiation, and chemicals and chemicals, potentiate or enhance each other; the human liver, for example, has an enzyme that helps protect it from malathion, but this enzyme is deactivated by other organic chemicals.

The children of Woburn, Massachusetts, where two wells had been tainted with trichloroethylene (also in the ground at Ocean County, at Denzer & Schafer, Ciba-Geigy and Reich Farms), developed high rates of seizure disorders. So have the children of the Ukraine and other parts of Russia after Chernobyl, the Russian nuclear power plant that melted down in 1986. The children of Chernobyl have also begun showing high levels of schizophrenia. Poisoning with lead, which shut down some of the Beachwood/Berkeley Wells, creates epileptic disorders too.

Manic-depression is a sophisticated seizure disorder, one that, like the response of the bees, makes the mind thrash in a frenzy of physical emotion. Mine probably began life as the petit mal, a sign that the circuits couldn't speak to one another the way they should.

The brain works on a complicated system of neurotransmitters—

chemicals—that tell the neurons to give off electrical impulses. Too many, you're overstimulated or manic: too few, understimulated or depressed. Once your brain cells learn to misfire they'll keep doing it; this is *kindling*, which is why a dose or two of a neurotoxin can leave brain function altered forever. Something walks into your mind and throws the lights on, and then they throw themselves on, over and over again.

Neurons look like a cross between regular cells and spider webs: spreading their wet nets out.

Once I went to the opera and heard a singer sing the top note of *"Mi chiamano Mimi"* in such a limpid glassy tone that my brain lit up. There's no other way to say it: my skull starred, a supernova. I was out of myself.

I wrote in my diary about a seizure, maybe drug induced, I had at fifteen:

> I went into some kind of fit earlier tonight. I was in my bedroom on the bed when all of a sudden all my muscles went all tense & tight & I was paralyzed, couldn't even move my mouth to scream. It lasted a few minutes. (8/19/72)

The neurotransmitter GABA, which is the traffic cop of neuro-transmitters, directing and regulating them, is stimulated by depakote and similar seizure-inhibiting drugs, and so can stabilize a brain system that has been disrupted.

Autism, which has no satisfactory medical explanation, can be treated with depakote.

Ocean County has a history of disease clusters of the brain and central nervous system: first the childhood cancers, then autism. Widespread contamination with toxic chemicals, especially organophosphate chemicals, is the theory now for the cluster of autistic children in the county.

The dump sites in Ocean County—Reich Farms, Dover Township Landfill, Ciba-Geigy—are pools of toxic chemicals, including pesticides: DDT; chlordane, like DDT but deadlier (2.5 parts per million of chlordane in the body will cause death to liver cells); organophosphates like aldrin (which even in small quantities leaves birds, rats and dogs infertile) and dieldrin. These lie alongside industrial chemicals like toluene and benzene, carcinogens, many of these chemicals potentiating one another. They block oxidation, inhibit the function of vital organs like the brain and adrenal system, cause cell death and attack the genome within the cell.

The Human Genome Project, run by the Department of Energy and the National Institutes of Health, has mapped the chromosomal site that holds the gene for manic-depression. It's on chromosome eighteen, midpoint, at the waist of the pronged chromosomal hourglass. Chromosomes hold our individual map—a map that gets smudged with use—coded in the amino acids of DNA. My mother and father, my grandparents, my greatgreatuncle the wrecker of ships: all reduced to information. In dominant and recessive genes, explaining both who you could have been and who you are.

Somewhere there's a chromosome holding a need—unvoiced—to make shipwrecks and drownings.

Radiation breaks chromosomes, like a woodchopper flailing at logs; broken chromosomes may reattach in disordered sequences, or pieces may be lost. These losses create damaged genes, and also allow defective recessive genes to become expressed, as their healthy dominants fly off.

My grandfather was a depressive man. His mother sounds like she had manic fits—hypersexual, impulsive, narcissistic—though not the rapid-cycling epileptiform fits I have and I think Mark has. Two other of the cousins suffer from severe depression.

My doctors loved my family history. They felt they wrestled with my genes, like characters in the Old Testament wrestling spirits. They knew me as someone born with seven demons inside. Though there's a lot written about the neurological and physical effects of chemicals and radiation I've never met a doctor who liked to talk about that.

A Department of Environmental Protection researcher named Judith, a woman assigned to Ocean County, told me, "It's heartbreaking. Everyone wants me to explain what's wrong with them."

I don't expect anyone to explain what's wrong with me. No one can explain what's wrong with anybody, I don't think. Though I don't believe in coincidences of this magnitude either: clusters of children with brain disorders, toxic plumes and clouds, radiation spewing in the air. Every vital system of my body disrupted: an arrhythmic heart, a seizing brain, severe allergies, useless reproductive organs. Either it's Sodom and this is the wrath of God or it's the wrath of man, which is thoughtless, foolish and much more lasting.

Their corsets glowed. Heavy enough to stand on their own, torsos like marble Aphrodites, spirit women. The hourglass, the womanness.

The five Radium Girls who'd irradiated their own clothes did something no one like them had done before: in 1927 they took U.S. Radium to court. Thousands of women had performed the same job but a lawsuit seemed farfetched—at the time no body of law said an employer owed employees workplace safety—so only these five tried to litigate. Everything about them got examined many times: hair, clothes, bodies. They died throughout the trial. They had nothing as subtle as cancer but radium sickness, not cell mutation but cell death. First their teeth fell out, their hair. Their jaws abscessed and their bones decayed, killed from the inside. Doctors supplied by U.S. Radium diagnosed syphilis and other things, like phosphorus poisoning.

Marie Curie, the pioneer of radium science, read about the case. She was appalled at conditions in the factory; in France, she said, radium workers used protection. She recommended the Girls eat raw liver to strengthen their blood and shook her head. (*There's no means for destroying the substance once it enters the human body*) In the courtroom the five were too weak to raise their hands to take the oath.

A few interested doctors exhumed the bodies of other dead dial painters. One dug up the body of a young Italian immigrant, whose death certificate had said "syphilis," and wrapped her cankered jaw in unexposed film. In a week it carried the print of her radioactivity.

The Girls won $10,000 each and an annuity, money that went to their survivors, and helped create the concepts of safe workplaces and environmental medicine. A decade later Marie Curie died of radiation-induced leukemia.

World War II broke out soon after the death of Madame Curie: the mother war, spawning such a tough-lived generation of little wars: the Cold War, the war on bugs and weeds, the war waged by industry on any substance that couldn't be altered by things found in nature.

The small war of nuclear power plants, born of the bomb and the promise of control of all that power.

When my good doctor first prescribed depakote, my husband brought me in. I was still a new patient of hers, and she'd been casting around for what to do, unhappily renewing prescriptions for a drug called verapamil—a holdover from my last doctor. I'd called Bruce in his office at graduate school, sobbing and babbling, telling him our house had filled with poison gas and my brain was on fire. He found me on the front doorstep and got an emergency appointment.

After a week or two on depakote something—some thrashing thing—snapped off.

I go several days without sleeping & the something huge is growing (7/5/87, age 30)

It has everything to do with light. And sleep. With the brain kindling like the sea at night, a huge swell of phosphorescence. Or turning off, a nothing, an undertow.

Periods of normalcy and then.

I know to worry if I quit sleeping. Two nights without sleep and I need to play with meds (that teenager still, rearranging her own consciousness). My record: one month of no sleep whatsoever. I lolled through the night with a wild party going on in my head: voices, lights, movement. My thoughts fragmented. I don't remember it well; I don't remember the poison gas episode at all. Like a drug stupor.

I just remember my house at night, learning the low almost sexual cry Bruce gave out when sleep came on him. What announces itself with the sun gone and the lightbulbs out—the glowing red digital clock, the watch flaring up at a button push, cats' eyes, blue X-ray glow of television in the dark.

Mania is about memory. It crowds your head because there's too much there to begin with and in mania you remember all of it at once. One night I recalled, looming intact in front of me, page after page of a book I read in fifth grade called *Cheaper by the Dozen*.

The mother in the book, I read, called rude things "eskimo."

"Don't say that. That's eskimo," she snapped at her children if they said "God."

I didn't want to know that detail. I had to spend the rest of the night wondering why *eskimo.*

Mania starts out exhilarating and ends in panic. First a smoldering horror—like the gas—then depression. The bubble collapses; it has to collapse. Once after a long high period I smashed my dishes. I've torn page after page from my journals, feeling like I could erase myself from the world they represented. Depressed, I become to myself an intolerable idea.

At eighteen I became a human being again. I'd quit street drugs at seventeen, and began facing the drugs I could not control. My brain chemicals, and the chemicals given by legal prescription. Before I had swallowed a mind, a place to be and a way to be: *goofy pills, silly-cybin, ups, downs.* I missed that—the absoluteness of the claim, of the follow-through. Pharmaceutical names have the same lushness, the same emotional hope, maybe a faint thrill of Greek tragedy—*thorazine, depakote.* Two warriors that ring the walls of Troy. Sometimes a cynical implication of relief: *soma, halcyon, elavil.* Less truth in advertising.

When I tell my doctor about my adolescence she dismisses it with a rake of her hair. "That's easy," she says. "You were self-medicating."

Depakote, which I've taken for nine years now, is a small pink oval, sweetish-smelling, not like candy but like dusting powder. Like something that, at the age of nine or ten, I'd have brought my grandmother in a pale canister. I'm told the sweet coating masks a nauseating flavor.

Depakote treatment's been the kind of success that makes other people call you a *different person*. Which I am, a blend of me and its chemical underpinning, valproate: a depakote person. Which worries me in some ways: when I say "myself" I lie by simplification. My thoughts are medicated thoughts. Of course, in mania I was not myself. In depression, people say, I am not *myself*. What exists, in the hum of that word? Depakote, little pink eucharist. The real eucharist, a chip of divinity. Hourglass chromosomes and threads of DNA; subdividing more, the adenine, guanine, thymine and cytosine—the four bases of the genes, swinging in their nineteenth-century blousy white cottons, their square suits, Bermuda shorts, in their peplums and Capri pants and pillbox hats.

There are the viruses I've had and my ancestors have had; viruses enter your DNA and resequence it. There's the pit lined with plastic and sludge, the slow clouds of DDT, the water my uncle had to take home because it had become part of his family.

The alpha rays, the beta rays, the gamma rays. The free radicals radiation and toxins make in the body, like hydroxyl—unstable oxygen molecules minus an electron. Hydroxyl will enter the molecular structure of DNA and take what it needs and leave another you.

I am, said the Buddha, is a vain thought. *I am not,* said the Buddha, is a vain thought.

Catherine of Siena said to God, "I am she who is not, and you are he who Is." I've always admired her, having lived in her city for a while—Siena, a walled city on a hill, a medieval city in Italy. A country many poor people left so they could go to another place and eat radium. Where Catherine, like Mary, has become a stained glass window, a woman who cut off her hair so she'd never have to marry, now glowing white and blue and emerald, mouth open, so the light goes through her, and also she swallows it.

Chapter Twelve

Self-Portrait in a Nuclear Mirror

To think we've gone and created immortality and the problem is how to mortalize it again. That we've not been able to make immortality for our bodies but have given them growths, splotches, sarcomas, melanomas, blastomas, calcifications, lesions*—

_____

*Myelomas, fibrocysts, toxic adenomas

things to cut away and look for and then cut away again. We grow superbacteria, retroviruses, breastless women. But we've bombarded simple ores with atomic bits and filled them with radioactivity, something that lives as close to forever as we can imagine. We've made immortality for our waste, which grows larger and more important and more alive, and bulks itself out to inhabit the spaces we dwindle ourselves away from.

Half-lives, half of a span our cryonics can only dream of: plutonium-239, 50,000 years; cesium-135, 6 million years; uranium-238, 10 billion years.

Oh excellent! I love long life better than figs.

The thing is if we can make immortality we're gods and if we're gods then nothing will ever be better than we can make it and here we are, sick gods, stuck with ourselves, and our lumpy, diminishing forms.

The radionuclides 90Yttrium,137mBarium, 103mRuthenium, 95mNiobium are known as daughters. They're each the child of a longer-lived radionuclide of the same name. Radionuclides bear only female children, at least in language, and are astonishingly prolific. Radionuclides come from fission and atomic decay, from elements changing as their atomic structure changes. Half-lives measure the time it takes them to become half as radioactive and can range from a few seconds to millions of years. As they throw off atomic bits radionuclides decay into other elements: fertile children, daughters.

Our Department of Energy plans to bury these radionuclides together, much of the nuclide waste vitrified into radioactive glass—liquid waste dried into powder, then mixed with glass materials and fused—at the crest of Yucca Mountain, Nevada. Borers and dynamite sleek out the insides of the bricky rock, even now. There the nuclides will continue to outlive us, frozen in their hundred miles of underground tunnels and doing nothing to disturb the regnancy of their parent-gods, if our plans for their immortality work out.

Most of this waste will be used fuel rods, bundles of uranium cylinders bombarded with neutrons to create fission. These rods hang suspended in the core of nuclear power plants, inside many layers of containment. The intense heat generated by their fission turns water into steam and powers turbines for inexpensive energy. Fuel rods last about six years and then must be replaced, still dangerously radioactive. Spent rods first go to rest in enormous bathtubs built into the plants, giant swimming pools filled with water tinted bright blue by the addition of the chemical boron, which absorbs neutrons and helps minimize unwanted fission. Because of the boron the pools glow absurdly azure, like the backyards of Hollywood moguls or the laps of luxury hotels. The reactor cores glow the same color, an unreal blue, the color of wealth or heaven.

A power plant's spent fuel storage is designed to have core offload capacity—in addition to holding the plant's used rods, the storage should be large enough to hold all the fuel rods currently firing the core. This allows the core to be dismantled if the need to repair it arises, or in the event of disaster.

Typically, old power plants run through their storage capacity and have little ability to build more: and neither the ability nor the desire to shut down. The swimming pools darken with dormant bodies. At Oyster Creek, the plant's holding tank filled to capacity sometime in the early 1990s. Around 1992 the plant ditched its core offload capacity and gave that over to the used rods that kept coming inexorably from the hot watery center, and now that's gone and the stored rods are being reracked, jammed in even closer together, closer than the original design specs say is safe, in the absurd Shangri-la boron blue.

Because there are many Oyster Creeks around there's Yucca Mountain. It's an astonishing idea: a creation story. The waste repository will hold most of the radioactive waste ever made in the United States, 25,000 tons stored right now at our 112 nuclear power plants, 77,000 tons by 2010. Most from nuclear power plants, some from nuclear weaponry. Let loose, this much radioactive material could send a nuclear cloud into the atmosphere that would cause everyone on earth to die of cancer, different cancers depending on what rays or atomic particles come to us and where they reach and the vulnerable cells in our body, each of us dying a perfect death tailored to who we are.

So we plan to shovel this waste into the earth and seal it and leave it there.

If you could hold in your hand a piece of the cylindrical black glass that is vitrified radioactive waste and look into it at your own face, you would see yourself (it shines well) in that smoggy, outlined way you see yourself in the paint job of a dark well-polished car. It would not be as good as a regular mirror but the longer you looked the more you'd notice detail, the sweep of your eyelashes, the dark of your nostrils, the pupils of your eyes—things that gain in importance in a black reflectant. If you looked at yourself in the black glass through the lens of an atomic microscope you'd see that in the pool holding your face the tight orderly hoops of atoms sometimes sent off flying particles, like bubbles shooting upward in a glass of soda. Then if you kept looking you'd see the unraveling take place not just in the surface holding up the image of your face but in your face itself, all those atoms beginning to fission, their neutrons flying, electrons flying so your hydrogen atoms, which should have one electron circling the nucleus, might have two or three or wear nuclei shaking naked with zero. Your beautiful rings (this is what electron paths would look like, they move so fast) with the bundles at the center would lapse into chaotic arcs and frantic knots. This would happen everywhere, in the eyelashes, the dark of your nostrils, the pupils, all the places that had become important. And you could watch this carefully, because the black glass is extraordinarily smooth and shiny and polished in its surface, for as long as it took you to die of the unraveling.

Without the microscope (though who knows? they could become as common as glasses someday), this possibility—of people wandering in and becoming transfixed by the hidden corridors and steel drums and the dark, innocent, secreted mirrors—has concerned builders of the Yucca Mountain Waste Repository so much that a new field of study has emerged. It looks for ways to tell people in the year 11,997 to stay the hell away from someplace: *transeonic communications.*

Danger! Poisonous Radioactive Waste Buried Here.
Do Not Dig or Drill Here Before a.d. 12,000.

This is the sign in use now, accompanied by a face that signifies, as much as any artist can make it obvious and universal, nausea. A preliminary sketch has been accepted, a man's head, hairless (why? fallout?), mouth open and nose puckered and upper lip retracted in clear sickness, eyes shut.

Munch's *The Scream* face, with its hands at its ears, still gets tossed around as an alternative.

Of course, 10,000 years ago humans had barely reached the Neolithic age, a few thousand years from learning to cultivate plant foods, fumbling with an invention called rope. We can't imagine how these people talked or thought. If the millennia-old horses scratched into the caves at Lascaux try to tell us something, we don't know what. Ten thousand years from now, there will be no English, or Chinese or Tagalog, as we know it.

It's a question of where on the pendent of time we're hanging, on this neck of history: we beacon a little at the future but we too are silenced, by our position and our strangeness. If time were a rosary we would be somewhere in the Five Sorrowful Mysteries, trying to speak to the Glorious Mysteries ahead.

One idea for Yucca Mountain came from a landscape architect: an enormous field of thorns, the thorns shaped from concrete and each one thirty-three feet high, surrounding the repository: a crown of thorns in the desert, to bolster an unintelligible prophecy. Then people argued that a civilization, seeing the field as art, might want to dig it up and move it. And then the crown of thorns would be gone and the people who dig might well be gone.

It's a question: how to communicate with a people you can't, by definition, understand, because they live in the incomprehensible future. Engineers keep coming up with ideas "on the model of Stonehenge": right now they're planning twenty-two feet high monoliths with warnings engraved in seven languages. Of course, if the builders of Stonehenge had been trying something similar they would have failed miserably, with that site's swarms of picnickers, its Snickers bars, empty boxes of McVittie's and UHT milk and Kodak litter. How do we keep them from doing what they're made to do, these radionuclides, these parents and these daughters?

———

I was at Stonehenge with my father. It was 1975; I had cleaned up. I had also quit writing—no journals since the overdose. My own life had exhausted me by then; I think I couldn't stand having even that much existence. I cloistered myself, refusing to talk to Kenny and my old friends. I worked jobs that didn't require too much skill—typing and secretarial jobs; I was always a good typist—paid my parents rent, and read, and read. I read historical fiction by Daphne du Maurier and romances I borrowed from aunt Catherine and a book of Wallace Stevens's I found in a used book store, and Shakespeare, and Sylvia Plath, who I learned about from *Ms.* magazine. I hunted up clues for who I could be next.

Around the Stonehenge time, I had gotten a General Equivalency Diploma and started classes at a community college. College scared me because I had so little time in school after eighth grade—I couldn't remember writing a paper, taking a test. But I finally decided I wanted to do it, having struck up an unlikely love affair with books. I liked being a quiet person who read. My closest friend there was an older woman named Joan, who'd left her husband for another woman. She read my papers and helped me write coherently, and mothered me, having me over to her and her lover's boxy suburban house for brownies.

My parents and I spoke again—back to the spare, cryptic language that had preceded my drug aphasia. We spoke Cassill. We talked about nothing with a certain kind of fluency.

Stonehenge that day was eerie and mobbed with people, backing up to the standing stones and getting their pictures taken just far enough away so their puniness would show. No one saw a standing stone without commenting on how many of himself it could contain, as if we'd all flocked there to disappear. It never occurred to me that the stones might have been a warning, to stop taking pictures of my father under their somnolent heights. To get away.

My father always demands I take his picture. "One more, for my sister," my father was probably saying. "For Pop. For Auntie. For Uncle Sal."

We came to England to visit my brother, who like me is always fleeing. He had a scholarship to go to school there, in Reading. I remember the Stonehenge day as picturesque, unlike the rest of that June, sunny and puffy; the weather had deserted any local allegiances and placed itself squarely in our corner. Cumulus clouds wafted on the lintels—the horizontal stones sleeping on the sarcens, the uprights. I walked around reading graffiti on the sarcens: *Justin + Jessica.* Sometimes one name scratched out by a deep cut. The background noise I imagine was the same as any tourist spot in England; flat American accents complaining about the quality of English meat.

My father pursued me with the Kodak saying, "One more. One for cousin Tony and little Tony." My mother followed him saying, "The druids, the druids, the druids."

I wonder if something seeped into our feet. Not just our feet but the feet of the millions who'd been to Stonehenge over time. Maybe just a desire, to take things apart, split them, move them around.

When I do or say something that disappoints my father, which is pretty much every time I talk to him, he says, "No you don't. Not my daughter." This was true before the drug period, during it and after.

My dad might add, "I know my daughter better than that." I quit arguing with him when I realized that a third person really does exist in this equation, one who only my father is aware of: my father's daughter, who stands in relation to me as a prior part of the amoeba, something I was born into and spread out from like a peduncle, and finally pinched off from and left. My father's daughter pre-exists me and can't be gotten rid of, since in the time before I learned to speak we were indistinguishable.

> I do think they have become simpler, who were once the Olympian athletes of disappointment, who could be disappointed facing all the possible endings of human life. Once they made the mistake of letting a dream take shape, develop hands & feet, grow a human face, & cry. But the shapelessness of the dream left a space around its body that shadowed it, & at graduations, weddings, celebrations, they watched the shadow. (7/16/89)

I wrote this journal entry at the age of thirty-two, staying in Italy for the summer. I'd gone back to school to get a graduate degree, a Master of Fine Arts in poetry. I had gotten a BA about eight years before, transferring my community college credits to Oberlin, which I picked by going to a library and making lists of schools with undergraduate creative writing programs, and deleting any with distribution requirements. I knew from looking at college textbooks that anyone with one year of high school would flunk the most basic college-level math and science courses.

Anyway, when I wrote the above I'd gone on to a graduate program and begun keeping a journal again. I had started writing one a few years before, in Italy, but it only lasted a few months, and in graduate school I started up again with a lot of new self-consciousness. Whatever my flaws, I had begun to try to come to terms with my parents: with their chronic dissatisfactions, with my father, whom I loved still, though with a love that couldn't find its way to reason.

it's like loving a phantom limb (7/11/89, age 32)

Love, I'm convinced, is something that exists outside of us, a part of
nature, like the sunlight. It is as impossible to bring it to bear on day-
to-day life as it is to force the sun to shine because you want to have
a picnic. (7/5/87, age 30)

I drive my father crazy. When I do the stuff he claims he wants me
to do I drive him craziest. If I walk into a room where my father's sitting and there's no one else to deflect my presence, he leaves. I'm like
a wandering electron colliding into his proton charge.

My dad has always been a phenomenally cautious man, unwilling
to drive for an hour without having his engine and tires checked, a full
tank of gas and the route mapped out. He's an accountant who saves
and hoards. He worries. He's a small, skinny man whose body always
seems to be shrinking off with worry. If you drive he screams warnings about cars lanes away. If he drives he screams and swears about
the assholes he says don't care if they kill him. The adrenaline can
destroy his stomach for days.

I will quit a job and move across the country out of boredom. I
spend. I eat. I stay up late at night and sleep and love pleasure. Even
when there's plenty to worry about I don't worry. My body's falling
apart and I don't worry. I have thrown over several lucrative careers
and do nothing to help myself, to ingratiate myself to higher-ups. I
have a houseful of animals, mostly strays I dragged home from one
place or another, who rat up the furniture and occasionally piddle on
the rug. I've been burglarized and rarely remember to lock up.

My father's a dapper man. Every morning of every day of his life, or
what of it I've been privy to, he has taken his kinky blueblack hair
(now gray) and oiled it with Vitalis into two marcel waves, undulating
outward from a center part. For the rest of the day his hair sits still and

glistening. His smell is the perfumed and the medicinal: Vitalis, Jade East, Noxzema.

I often go years between haircuts and don't bother untangling my hair, though I have a habit of grabbing a knot and teasing it apart with my fingers, dropping torn hairs all over the floor, while I'm thinking.

I crash into his life like a physical rebuke, like Job's boils.

Because my father loves me he hates me; he feels the need to protect his daughter from this strange, slovenly, reckless, careless other woman.

Still we cannot quit talking (on the phone—we don't talk in person) in a disembodied dialectic of need and complaint.

My mother, who's deaf, answers. *(Mary. Pick up.)*

When I get across to her that it's me she murmurs a few things, hands the phone to my father.

"I thought you would of called."

"I am calling."

"Sooner I mean."

"I called Wednesday. It's Saturday."

My father's voice turns plaintive. "I have sinus."

Everywhere my father goes he has little foil packets and spray cans of over-the-counter medicines—nasal sprays, Tylenol, Sudafed, Sinutab, Tums, Pepto-Bismol, for the head, throat, sinuses, gut disorders he claims to have perpetually.

My father feels like no one listens. He feels no one understands the complaints of his body. Ever mindful of his mortality, he feels no one else is *(I could go any day, you know)*. His is an Old Testament voice, crying in the wilderness. Unaware maybe that immortality has been made, that it's hushed and waiting underground in the desert.

"A *new thing* had just been born; a new control," I. I. Rabi said of the first bomb test. Like Michelangelo's ceilinged God we stretched out our hands. And brought them back burning. Different, atomically charged. Like the incarnation: when God took on the flesh of his creation.

Adam: from Hebrew, "earth." *Atom,* from Greek, "do not cut."

It meant withdrawing to desert secrecy, the sun and the humility of sand, with its billions of dispensable members.

In the 1940s, during the war, J. Robert Oppenheimer brought Enrico Fermi and six thousand assorted others—physicists, workers and families—to the New Mexico desert and formed the Los Alamos labs to create and build the atomic bomb. This was the Manhattan Project. Fermi came from Rome, a refugee from Italian fascism, and Oppenheimer was the son of immigrants, German Jews. They came like immigrants, seeing utopianism and land. They slapped together Los Alamos the way my grandfather threw up our bungalows: board cottages, water that half the time didn't run and all the time wild games of chance.

The whole group partied at night at Los Alamos, with punch spiked with 200-proof lab alcohol ("It was a lark," says the physicist Freeman Dyson. People had "the time of their lives.")

The Los Alamos crew called the bomb the "gadget."

The thing is, we built the bomb to take out Germany. German scientists had split the atom. The Allies spent the early part of the war terrified that Hitler might develop atomic power. Einstein wrote to Roosevelt about it, a letter warning, "This new phenomenon [fission] would also lead to the construction of bombs, and it is conceivable— though much less certain—that extremely powerful bombs of a new type could thus be constructed." But Germany never figured out how to use fission power, and before the Los Alamos scientists had solved the problem of how to build a nuclear bomb Germany surrendered.

German soldiers crossed the fields with their hands behind their heads, and the justification for Los Alamos surrendered. Why go on? A Los Alamos scientist named Robert Wilson thought about it a little and hosted an evening discussion called "Effect of the Gadget on Civilization." Thirty of the six thousand at Los Alamos came.

Frank Oppenheimer, J. Robert's brother, who also worked on the bomb said dreamily, "We all kept working because the machinery had caught us."

The Los Alamos crew cogged in their wheels toward the world's first bomb test, in July 1945, in a part of the desert called Jornada del Muerto (Dead Man's Journey). Oppenheimer named the test "Trinity," after a line in a poem he'd been reading by John Donne: "Batter my heart, three person'd God . . ." Donne's poem was a plea for God to take him, and maybe Oppenheimer's test was an answer.

On July 16, at Dead Man's Journey, also called Alamogordo, the first nuclear bomb went off.

> The effects could well be called unprecedented, magnificent, beautiful, stupendous and terrifying. No manmade phenomenon of such tremendous power had ever occurred before. . . . It was that beauty the great poets dream about but describe most poorly and inadequately.
> *(Brig. Gen. Thomas F. Farrell, at Trinity)*

> All vegetation had vanished. . . . The effects on the tower indicate that, at that distance, unshielded permanent steel and masonry buildings would have been destroyed. I no longer consider the Pentagon a safe shelter from such a bomb.
>   The test was successful beyond the most optimistic expectations.
> *(General Leslie Groves, builder of the Pentagon and military head of the Manhattan Project, at Trinity)*

Everyone spoke at once after the test, though everyone was temporarily deafened.

Before the Trinity test the Los Alamos people forged a secret plan for evacuating the state, with the help of the military and the governor. The physicists discussed the remote but real possibility that the test would explode the atmosphere and destroy the planet. During the actual explosion Enrico Fermi took bets on whether the state of New Mexico would be destroyed.

A Los Alamos memo dated July 14 read, "Gadget complete. Should we have the chaplain here?"

Atom meaning "do not cut."

Trinity was, in a strange way, the day of my birth. When the bombs fell on Hiroshima and Nagasaki, in August 1945, my father slept on a barge in the harbor of San Francisco. (We bombed Japan because "all the bureaucratic apparatus existed to do it," says Freeman Dyson. "It would have taken a president with an iron will not to.")

My father was in the Navy, a skinny eighteen-year-old who in photos looks like a twist of pipecleaners inside his Navy bellbottoms. He read sonar, studying blips for signs of submarines. He slept on a barge while his destroyer, the *U.S.S. Emory*, got refurbished.

If the bombs hadn't been dropped he would have been in the first wave of standard military attacking Japan.

"You wouldn'ta had your father," he says. "We wouldn'ta survived the KAMmy-kays."

"The what?"

"KAMmy-kays." His voice is frustrated, insistent.

I get it finally. "Oh. Kamikazes."

For once my father's sense of his own mortality is right. The first wave of U.S. military was expected to be massacred, though the loss of life would have been lower than the deaths due to the atomic bombs—

200,000 for both cities, and an untold number later from cancers, leukemias and other radiation diseases. After the bombs dropped many
thousands of pregnancies miscarried; the chromosomal damage of
radiation destroys the fetus.

I was born under a cloud, or in one, a fluke. Like many of my
friends, like Robin, whose father winged his way to Hawaii to join the
Japanese invasion when the bombs fell. The daughter of my father,
who did not die in the Sea of Japan because we had the bomb, and was
the substitute for my mother's intended husband, Angelo, who died at
Normandy because we did not yet have the bomb. We are the creatures
of an alternate reality created in the New Mexico desert—a vision had
by men still exploring this country, a vision where Americans lived
and others died.

Of course, in many cultures—Yoruba, Shinto, old Hebrew—my
father is dead anyway, lost through the loss of a continuing line of
bodily offspring.

Radiation is the alpha and omega of our lives, the beginning and
the end.

My father often refers to himself as "your father." It is probable my
father is as much a mystery to him as his daughter is to me.

There's a smaller version of Yucca Mountain. It received its first nuclear
waste shipment in mid-1999 and so is our country's first permanent
holder of nuclear waste. It lies near Carlsbad, New Mexico: WIPP, the
Waste Isolation Pilot Plant. Around it, like a Stonehenge, loops a fence,
a sarcen of signs. It has the billboard with the bald almost puking head,
and the warnings to stay away until A.D. 12,000. WIPP's relatively
small, carved into ancient saltbeds 1,200 feet below the New Mexico
desert. Fifty-six rooms—one, I can't help thinking, for each year of

the century before I was born. The repository holds only weapons waste, what we've generated since the 1940s—mostly things contaminated with plutonium: metal fragments, clothes, rubber shoes, rags.

The detritus of Fat Man and Little Boy, the Hiroshima and Nagasaki bombs, rest in those salt chambers, if you can call that subterranean seething rest.

WIPP's builders chose the location for its proximity to Los Alamos, still an active nuclear weapons lab. Edward Teller built the hydrogen bomb at Los Alamos—the one dropped at the Bikini atoll; it proved to be one thousand times more powerful than the bomb dropped on Hiroshima (the cloud "looked like a diseased brain, like the brain of a madman," said an onlooker). In the 1990s American nuclear secrets leaked from Los Alamos to the Chinese, who designed and built a set of nuclear warheads from American plans.

Chris and I call my father Poobah. Chris saw a little of the Gilbert and Sullivan operetta *The Mikado* one night flipping channels, and named my father after a character who's mayor, judge, jury, police and executioner. We call my mother Mothra, a nickname I came up with, after a Japanese monster movie where radioactivity breeds a giant mutant moth. Weirdly affectionate, that we've always used nicknames for my parents, and reflective of the fact that they seem like anything but a mother and a father.

"Poobah," I phone him. "How are you?"

"I have a cold."

"A new cold?"

"The same cold." A pitch higher. "I thought you would of called to find out how I'm doing!"

Poobah. How are you? You brought me into a world that could be already dead.

But my cold!

We built this thing that could've ended the world. Maybe it did end the world. Maybe our brain cells are fissioning through the atmosphere.

But you don't talk about the cold! You don't ask.

When I think of my father I think of bread. Real bread, the kind we drove Route 22 to buy at Poppalardo's in Little Italy and Giordano's in Newark, long tough loaves with blurred smiles where the knifeslash grows apart in baking, and round loaves covered with knobs of dough. Primordial bread. When I started moving around, my father visited me with shopping bags filled with loaves. He knew I missed the kind of bread I grew up eating in New Jersey, bread baked by Italian immigrants who built their own Italian ovens from imported tile long before bread got trendy and profitable, out of pure nostalgia.

Now that bread's become fashionable and pricey my Puget Sound town has four or five great bakeries and my father goes out every morning foraging, at six o'clock. When we get up white bags and square white bakery boxes unfold across the table, with rustic Italian and dark rye and seed bread, and sweet rolls with pecans, cinnamon twirls and scones.

"Do you like the cinnamon twirls?" my father asks anxiously. "Do you like the seed bread? I counted seven kinds of seeds. There's this one, this one, this one, this one, thisone, thisone, and thisone."

Then, plaintively, "I thought you'd never get up."

Though my father tells me I'm too plump he could happily sit until Armageddon buttering me slice after slice of bread.

My father says, "Nobody needs to sleep that much. You could train yourself out of it." He sees sleep as weakness. My mother shares these values: early rising, hard work, self-denial. Remembering your place, your female, laboring, nongenius place.

It occurs to me that my basic characteristics must come from somewhere, must come somehow from my father and my mother. That these are parts of themselves they've burnt off and I'm their Yucca Mountain, their waste repository, looking, from where they sit in time, like I'm ten thousand years.

My dad calls me and says, "Tell Jin about us." He's referring to my son. Bruce and I cut off fertility treatments—ignoring the doctor's plea for at least one try at in vitro "or we'd regret it"—and decided to adopt. Jin arrived at the age of five months: we drove to the airport with an empty carseat, and got a groggy, blackhaired, beautiful baby who filled it, and looked and looked at us in wonder. Full of questions, with no language. We brought him home, took baths together, nestled under our down quilt like measuring spoons. Jin learned he could nap on my stomach, and still does sometimes. For him I am loving furniture.

Jin was born in Korea. I don't know his mother. My father sent a check for $100 when Jin arrived and asked me to open him a bank account.

"Tell him about us," he said urgently. "Tell him we stand for saving."

We kept Jin's Korean name when we adopted him—it means "jewel" or "ore." We kept his other name, "Woo," which means "happy."

My grandparents, who spoke Italian and lived in an Italian neighborhood, named my father Nicola Giuseppe, a fact I learned from my Italian grandfather. My father's very uncomfortable with his birthname, and goes by Nicholas Joseph.

My father grew up mostly in East New York in Brooklyn; he had relatives on every floor, his grandparents at the top. My aunt Philomena was the only girlchild in the brownstone so his extended family installed a buzzer on her floor and rang it when they wanted menial jobs done, floors mopped, clothes ironed, dishes washed, tomatoes seeded and skinned. My aunt worked all day, running from apartment to apartment, and because her family needed her to this extent she never finished school. My aunt used to get disgusted and disconnect the buzzer and for that she got whipped though she claims not to be resentful of either fact. Her own mother, my grandmother, was sickly, her heart scarred. Because the family was poor my father went to work too, at the age of ten, selling *Liberty* magazines on streetcorners in Brooklyn.

My father made good. He entered the middle class. In fact, he's now upper-middle, thanks to his frugality and a talent for picking stocks. He became an accountant and saved and bought stock options whenever his company offered them, then sold those stocks for a profit and bought other stocks. When I was in my third year of college he and my mother moved away from the Elizabeth area and bought a very suburban splitlevel in that good address, Fanwood. My father realized the American Dream, the first one in his family to do so. His grandfather worked and his father dug and dug, ditches and graves, and never quite got his shovel into the right piece of earth, the one with the gold and coins and the treasure.

My father has told my brother he cannot die until I forgive him. He will ask my forgiveness on his deathbed. I will give it lovingly though if he recovers neither of us could go on to articulate what I forgave him for.

I've been a bad parent.
No.
I've been a bad parent.
All parents are bad parents.
Sometimes I made like you didn't exist.
I don't exist.

When the monoliths with the warnings in seven languages go up around Yucca Mountain they'll all say the same thing and linguists, we hope, will use one language to decode another, like we did with the Rosetta Stone. The signs will direct future people to an underground message center, with computer terminals and models and descriptions of the Waste Repository Project and requests to continue passing along Yucca Mountain's message.

We humans now are *Homo sapiens sapiens,* Man Wise Wise. Who knows who the next ones will be—*Homo sapiens sapiens sapiens,* or maybe the half-human, half-alien species the *Inquirer* keeps telling us about. I haven't read this in the plans but it seems irresistible not to include more information about us in the underground center. Apologies, day-to-day life stuff, descriptions of who we are that make us sound more appealing than 77,000 tons of radioactive waste.

If I were asked to pick a relic of our civilization to put in a time capsule I'd pick a particular brand of children's juice, one that comes in a tiny carton with a built-in straw. It's called juice and is labeled "Real, 100% Juice" to distinguish it from the many other things on the market called juice. To drive home its specialness the name of this product contains the word juice not once but twice: *Juicy Juice.* I'd crumple the carton up a little and throw it on the floor of the message center at Yucca Mountain. The people of the future could either get the point, and know everything about us they need to know, or dismiss my message as somebody's trash, in which case things would have changed so little what I have to say would be meaningless.

Maybe the Five Sorrowful Mysteries will have come round again.

Enrico Fermi and I share a birthday—September 29, Michaelmas, the feast day of St. Michael, patron saint of war.

My parents live frugally. They visit now and then and say they hate the flight, the cramped plane and bad food, and insist they can't afford to fly except coach class in budget carriers. They want us to come to them, just as we have to call them, on Sundays. My father believes in making people pull themselves up by the bootstraps, use elbow grease, sweat blood.

My father adds to Jin's savings account every now and then. It's still small but he's never told me what he'll add to it over time; he hints it may be everything he's got.

"You can't do anything with money, you and Chris," he says. He thinks we'd waste what he's worked for. As far as that goes he's right, at least in terms of his own definitions of wasting. Most of what my father's given me in life he's regretted, even my body, which I spoil, with wine and chocolate and sleep, and with real diseases and dysfunctions that afflict me as they never have him, and which he dimly suspects must be my fault somehow.

My father loves the idea of Jin having everything, as long as we can sit with the passbook and explain it to him, translate the rows of numbers and shares and dividends into a language that still, years and years from now, will deliver the message of my father.

This is what my father left you.

What he left me?
He left you numbers.
What numbers?
90. 138. 235. 50,000. 6 million.
A lot?
Enough to last.

Yucca Mountain begins with a lie. It was a lie before anyone planned to bury their eons' worth of damage there. It's a lie of words, of terminology, not a mountain at all but a desert ridge that looks like a long snake anchored by knobby ropes of butte, ruddy brown, composed of a volcanic ash called tuff. To store the waste successfully the area needs to be geologically dead, free of seismic activity.

There's not much yucca either, there's mostly nothing: six inches of rain a year and very low groundwater, which is why people think it may be a safe place to seal away these restless parents and their daughters.

WIPP has been designed to hold only what's called "pure" radioactive waste—waste uncontaminated with the industrial chemicals used in commercial fission plants. Yucca will take mixed waste—volatile organic chemicals, petrochemicals, fuel rods, poisoned radioactive sludges. It will be an infinitely concentrated version of Ocean County.

What your eye dwells on now at Yucca Mountain is the repository project as it's developed so far, three billion government dollars' worth of feasibility studies and preliminary drilling. You can see photos of it at several sites on the World Wide Web: mostly men in loose yellow uniforms looking meditative under enormous red rock, scooped in like a cantaloupe. Huge bores burrow into the mountainside; men cut rock with housesized saws. Long low barracks house engineers and experts and workers and border gaping openings in the rock wall, arched like the entrances to old coal mines or railroads, housing the start of the hundred miles of tunnels.

Fifty years after the last canister swims into the hold in the earth, guided by robots that will work in the intense radioactive atmosphere, the entrances will be sealed and Yucca Mountain the yuccaless ridge will be still and uninhabited, we hope, for ten to twelve thousand years. Though a fault, the Ghost Dance fault, runs through the repository, and a few miles away an Energy Department building shook with an earthquake and sustained $1 million in damage in June 1992. Fission will take place constantly inside the tunnels and the canisters themselves will lose atomic stability, and so will the ground itself. If water percolates upward through the ridge, as it could in the event of geological change, the groundwater will lose its atomic identity. Everywhere there will be freeroaming electrons, neutrons, sorrowful unfulfilled nuclei. The containers and the conveyor belts and the robots and the sand will become hot. People nearby will be dosed with radioactivity. If the groundwater ever reached the canisters the ridgetop would blow.

Yucca Mountain lies on Indian land, Western Shoshone and Paiute. A few miles away, at Jackass Flats, there's an old nuclear test site; we've always taken Indian land for nuclear experiments. The Ghost Dance Fault's named for an Indian movement, when tribes danced an ecstatic dance* they believed would rouse their ancestors into burying the whites who'd taken over their land, and bring back the open spaces and the buffalo.

One of the most immediate dangers of the Yucca Mountain Waste

---

*"Father I come/Mother I come/Brother I come
  Father, give us back our arrows"

Repository lies not in the mountain but in the way to it, the squirming path. The canisters will contain plutonium-rich fuel rods as well as plutonium from decommissioned nuclear warheads and other radioactive substances. One pound of plutonium, evenly distributed, would induce lung cancer in every human being on the planet. Of course, the waste in its deep bathtub sleep can't swim itself to Yucca Mountain, and the automated railroads that will deliver it inside the tunnels can't get it there. Trains and trucks will deliver all this radioactive waste to Yucca, through forty-three states, with somewhere between five hundred (government estimate) to three thousand (critics' estimate) deliveries a year to the ridge. Through New York, where Middle Eastern terrorists blew up the largest building in the country with a bomb in the parking garage, through Oklahoma City, where domestic terrorists used fertilizer to atomize a building containing hundreds of people and a daycare center; past San Francisco, where part of the elevated Nimitz Freeway collapsed in an earthquake.

Any of these disasters en route, or a seismic shift at WIPP or Yucca, could lead to a disaster much worse than Hiroshima and Nagasaki. It may matter less that we used the bomb than that we built it, and then allowed its technology to be borrowed by utility companies, to boil water and light lights.

My father has a temper. It feels of the earth: something moving and evolving in lower places that only becomes clear when it needs to rise. My brother and I and my mother always lived in fear of it. My father's temper could arise out of nothing; it seemed like a living thing that grew in him and when it ripened you could sense it traveling almost on the outside of his body. He needed to rage sometimes.

> He was yelling. (He called me "that girl over there.") Then he said the three of us could go to hell. (11/28/67, age 11)

I wrote this one night when Chris, my mother and me came home an hour late from my aunt's house, because we had to wait for an uncle to give us a ride. My father's temper descended on him like a sickness, or like a consciousness of sickness. He tore at us, trying to uncover his real flesh. I did not hate him for this. I too sensed the errors, the disparity between me and my father's daughter.

"You'd think I was an animal," my father says, listening to my brother and me reminisce about our childhood.

We'd gotten on the subject of my father's punishments, those punishments he thought so hard about and that rapt you out of your life in a way almost divine. Two weeks sitting on the side of your bed, no books or toys, eyes on the floor, thinking about your sins. As if someone were to make you by force a Desert Father. My brother used to get that punishment for sneaking over to play in the cemetery in Elizabeth.

"Is that what you're going to tell Jin?" my father wants to know.

I assure my father that that's not exactly what I'm going to tell Jin, at least not all I'll tell him.

Two children had died in that cemetery. They were murdered and left there and in one of those moments of irony in our ironic century men carted their bodies from the Evergreen, drained them of fluids, pumped them with new fluids and returned them respectfully to almost the same spot where they died. Pedophiles? Junkies? We never knew who did it. The children died in some way too ghastly for my parents to tell us at the time, and now they can't remember.

Nicola Giuseppe was born in 1926, in a world poised between the two Wars to End All Wars. His species had, just a few decades before, learned haltingly to fly. My mother, Mary Brenda, was born in 1920. Their earliest memories are of the Great Depression, money in bank vaults becoming like ash, a nothing thick with significance. My father's homes disappeared in the Depression. His grandparents had been peasants who did not know hospitals or planes or tractors or any real medical care. They died and gave birth at home, moaning simply.

My parents married in the 1950s, when cars were the size of nineties office cubicles, babies lolled on the laps of passengers who never clicked a seatbelt, everybody smoked. And tumbled their children out into the sixties and its revolutions: Women's Liberation, civil rights, the sexual revolution, soaring homicide, a new breed called serial killers. Computers, men in white puffy bodysuits tumblesaulting on the moon.

No wife of mine is going to work, my father said, and by extension no daughter.

My father tells me on the phone that feminists *(libbers)* have caused our divorce rates.

But there's not really much of a women's movement now, I tell him.

"They started all this crap," he insists.

Even now when my father's visiting if he hears me say, Your turn to do dishes, he says, "Oh Christ, this your turn, my turn, if I do this you do that, it makes me sick."

You libbers you wanted something.

So?

I'm trying to tell you. Look where wanting got me.

My parents visit to see my son. They're up-front about that: my father calls to say, "You know, we're not coming to see you." He laughs. It's important for him to establish this, that we're no longer the carriers of the future, the shining lamp. It's clear to me somehow that he loves

Jin much more for being adopted, not being his in the physical sense I am (guanine, thymine, cytosine, adenine). There is no grandfather's grandson to cast its shadow around this love. This may be true of my love for Jin as well, which is simple and besotted and has irritation sometimes but no rage. I'm not complaining. My parents are caring in their way—my father calls and rants about the Democratic President, whose evils he traces back to the sixties, and my mother sits with her piles of newspapers, clipping everything having to do with the Puget Sound area and mailing it to me, without comment.

There is cellular memory in mice, in flatworms: teach them something, their cells pass on the knowledge. You grind up the flatworms and feed them to one another, and mazes learned by the dead will hang in the memory of the living, *déjà vu*. Not that they know the tricks immediately but they learn them right away, unnaturally fast, and if you teach the first ones to go into the electric shock rather than away from it, the survivors will want to do that too.

My parents visit and our cells incline together and reminisce. We're quiet, a house full of cellular history: Gesualdo, Lincolnshire, St. Michael's Parish in Barbados where my family came in 1647, in chains (later the parish of the great Barbados Mental Hospital), and St. Andrew's Parish, where my greatgrandfather's home stood on the wild coastline over the Atlantic, on land that was pure rock.

All the water we drank, in a body-obliterating communion, from a well declared contaminated in the early eighties.

In spite of everything I know my father in his grudging way likes to see me, like I enjoy him, not his presence exactly but the detritus of his presence. We give my parents our bedroom, and I sneak in there to see the oak dresser with my father lined up on its bright surface: Prell, a leather traveling pouch, nail scissors, clippers, a small moustache comb, a round of sweet wax, black hair combs, Vitalis, Jade East, Dentyne, floss, foil packets of Tylenol Extra-Strength, Tylenol PM, sinus pills. The TV blasts in the morning the way it did when I was young: my father needs noise. My mother brings sacks of newspapers and goes out and gets more—anything, she'll read the worst local rags—and sits discarding layers of shed paper all around her, like a pupa perpetually molting.

We sit around watching my son eat and sleep and bang together his blocks and toy telephones. I've quit telling my parents anything I do, my writing or my recreation or my friends, all of which represent how I'm not living in New Jersey anymore, staying close and quiet, helping out, answering the buzzer.

In fact we barely speak. It's not like the telephone, where my father can articulate, somehow, the decades of losses that make up his life. I float past my parents like a bubble, a bubble carrying food for them, simple meals of bread and roast chicken, and diapers and baby bottles full of soy milk. My father says of Jin, "He's a good eater, God bless him."

And he says, looking at Jin, "I wonder if I'll be alive when he goes to school. When he goes to high school. When he gets his license." And on and on. It's become an obsession of his, to chart his extinction against my son's small and soft and fragrant body.

I work part-time and am home most of the day now. My time has become baby time: diapers, cooking and grinding food, reading aloud colorful and simple books. I have turned my life over. To me, Jin represents the end of the line: no more of the smugglers, men with replaceable wives, mothers who disappear into the sun. To my father and mother, of course, Jin represents continuance.

One day I pass my dad leaning over the high chair. I've come in with freshpicked raspberries for the baby. My father's bending over, his head framed by the halo of a silvery Mylar birthday balloon. I can hear him whispering. He's saying, "Remember these. These are my values." I don't know what he's been saying.

Sometimes I think: as little as I know my father Jin will know me. I'll bend over him, like the men at Trinity, a moving mouth.

Can you hear me?

No.

Can you hear me?

I'm a child.

Can you hear me?

Maybe I hear and I don't understand.

I need to tell you this, you've come to America.

And who knows what, of all we've left him, will reach him (we've worked at giving what we can)—reach him through the breath and through the mouth, through the soil at his feet, its own, secret breeding.

Epilogue

Specific Endpoints of Concern

It is the year two thousand. No question about this year except what to call the decade it begins: the *oughts*, the *naughts*. Soon we'll stand corrected or negated. Like all times this millennial year resembles the rest. One hundred and ten children have now been documented with cancer in Toms River. Jan Schlictmann (a lawyer played by John Travolta in the movies; more glitter filtering through the pines) has taken the case of several families with sick children, and filed suit against Ciba-Geigy.

This year a multinational called AmerGen bought the Oyster Creek Nuclear Generating Station. The reactor's spent fuel pools continue to grow beyond capacity and it has shutdowns, incidents, operator error reports several times a month; I belong to a listserv that sends me notices. Baby teeth continue to fill envelopes and sit under the scintillating counters. They twitch with picocuries of strontium-90 at levels matching those found in children during aboveground bomb testing back in the fifties and sixties.

The waste repository at Yucca Mountain continues to burrow into the ridge—five miles of it now—and the protest against it continues. Scientists at Cal-Tech and Harvard have found the earth's crust at Yucca moves faster than the DOE claimed, raising the chances of an earthquake; groundwater may move faster too. But $6 billion has been spent; no other sites looked at; and there's the waste, a city's worth—a whole race of new beings, alive and breeding—with no home.

The Radioactive Tooth Fairy, goldcrowned and hungry for more teeth, rode in a float in the last Toms River Halloween Parade.

My son's turned three and become a storyteller. He spins in the effortless way of children when they start mining their fantasies for myth. The stories are, he says, his memories—a narrative memory researcher John Kotre calls the ultimate myth ("Open the mind," writes Albert Goldbarth, "and the past it requires will surface").

All of Jin's stories begin, "Once" (*Once when I were a big boy*). It's the "once" that means there was a clear other history, like the Inuit time when humans and animals had no boundaries and each could become the other. Or the Greek time when gods and humans lived together simply, and came to each other's weddings and wars, sharing wishes and gossip and food.

Once, when you and Daddy weren't borned yet I did go to visit God at the North Pole.

Once, when you and Daddy weren't borned yet, me and uncle David found eyeballs in the closet but they was nice eyeballs.

Jin in his land before now lived with his uncle—morphed in that place to a brother—though he's only met this uncle once, and can't possibly remember him. Uncle David has his own problems; his seven-year-old Zach's been diagnosed with a virulent subtype of childhood leukemia. Last Christmas we called David's house and wellwished while Zach, bald from chemo and throwing up all day, cried in frustration in the background.

At first I loved that we were bringing Jin to Bellingham. Koreans venerate mountains and water: the place felt accurate for him. Then I read in our *Herald* that this area, like Toms River, has an abnormal rate of children with cancer. Raspberry fields in the county get heavy sprays of pesticides; we have one Superfund site containing creosote and chemicals that feeds a creek leading to our bay; and our Georgia-Pacific plant dumps mercury and chlorine. The heavy cumulus of the plant's steam emissions are ever-present, looking in a cloudy landscape like a small sky answering back the larger one.

Can we leave? Would that really be leaving? I always wonder what our further undoing will be, the gross unforeseeable errors: like the Romans, who baked lead into their ceramic tableware for the gloss. Testing at Pompeii found enough lead to have made the average Pompeiian sick or mad. As we do, the Romans saw danger everywhere and reached for protection: read the softlobed livers of sheep, sowed Carthaginian soil with salt. Then reclined to a hearty serving of their own destruction.

Jin's mythmaking started when he saw photos of Bruce and me before he came, before his birth *(Where Jin go?)*. It created a way for him to explain that uncomfortable void of time before existence. None of us likes that time. "Invisible are all things before birth," writes the Bhagavad Gita, which calls existence *being seen*. We don't like to be invisible. To me too Jin's nonexistence has become impossible; he's like an element or a celestial body I've discovered, whose hiddenness can't in any way change the huge gravity he's always cast.

Jin has asthma. It developed in his second year of life, in a country where the rate of asthma in children under five has increased 160% in the last fifteen years, to the point of being epidemic. In Jin asthma takes the form of one lung disease after another—bronchitis, pneumonia, each following the other. Until we got him to a specialist and began a routine of starting and ending each day by putting a yellowstriped rubber mask over his face and pumping drugs into it.

First we give him drugs by mouth, then steroid spray in the nostrils, then a bronchodilator and a steroid spray through the mask. He's learned to tolerate the routine but resents it, and so it's all stuff that didn't have to be done in that mythic time. The time before parents and their love brought this flesh and its walls.

Jin missed me then, he says. He wanted me to come, and waited and waited, and drove to the airport for me.

I take him to the water often. A pod of gray whales swam into our bay this year; they were starving, and we watched as they spouted and parted water with their slick backs. One stopped moving and drifted like a small island onto shore, dead, peaceful. I take Jin to see our orca whales, with their fierce binary markings, like Judgment Day. It's a news event when the orcas calve; PCBs and dioxins in our waters have made them more and more infertile; they miscarry, or don't conceive, or their weakened young die.

I fed my baby Jin formula that smelled of oats and chalk and coated a spoon like cream. I filtered his water, even to cook rice. Now he eats organic vegetables, freerange chemicalfree meats, everything made in our kitchen, maybe grown in our compostheavy yard.

He sings a song from Reader Rabbit: *From my head down to my feet/I'm made of things I drink and eat . . .*

When I feed him, in my mind we can't stay home. We eat at the edge of the water, or on the crux of Mt. Baker, that glows at sunset with the eerie sunset reflection—like a smoldering burn—called *alpenglow.* I take glacier or pebbles or whatever I can find (we do not have anything as kindly as sand beach here) and grind it into cereal; the white emissions from G-P catch like milk in my cups. I feed Jin this place. I feed him strips of the orcas with their body burdens and the sparse blubber of the starved whales. I hold dirt to his lips on the silver baby spoon my mother fed me with, the one that was hers as a baby, that has signs of the zodiac embossed on its looped handle. I can't help what I'm doing. This is all the food there is.

I help him fit into what the Bhagavad Gita calls the *new garment* of this life. Tailor, alterer: I must help him be seen.

Sometime around Halloween Jin wandered painting in the backyard, wearing an old plaid shirt of his father's that reached the ground, sleeves lopped off. He was sick, coughing to the point of vomiting with bronchitis, and bored. I bundled him and he went out back, barely visible outside of the shirt: three feet of sheer will. After a few minutes he left the four dull corners of his easel to paint the leaves on the withering raspberry canes. When I came out to see him he stood, painting desiccated leaves seagreen.

"It isn't right," he said to me ferociously. "It isn't right, they let witches fly through the air."

When I had my thyroid removed he curled in my lap after the surgery, playing with the plastic over my throat and pulling at the shunt, amused by the six-inch Mona Lisa smile of the incision across my neck. I'd been afraid it would scare him but it amused him instead, a new item for his mythological store of the normal: mothers with seeping wounds.

I pick up the paper one day and see an Associated Press story that says almost one-half of all Americans suffer at least one chronic disease. The figure, it says, is about 20 million higher than researchers predicted, and the number grows. Someone named Dr. Anderson at Johns Hopkins gives sound bites on this "major health challenge": we must study it, we must fight it. In my house we just toss the paper aside and get out of bed and begin our regimen of pills, inhalers, sprays and masks. Then we play hide and seek, or chase each other around, pretending to be monsters.

Here we are: Daddy monster, Mommy monster, green, clawed, vanishing, poking a thumb out from behind the door.

Here we're not: even these games don't happen in Jin's other world. In memory, that mythological place I climb out of for him, the one I once wanted to wrap in mud or clay for the future. In that parallel universe Jin waits in a giggly landscape of brother, God and freefloating eyes, for history, America, the birth of the nuclear, of his parents.

Acknowledgments

This kind of a book requires the help of so many people: thanks to Willie DeCamp, Dale Bridenbaugh, Dr. Wayne Landis, and all the groups like STAR and TEACH working with little reward to uncover what is really beneath and around us. Thanks to Rosina, a true friend of the heart, for her close reading and encouragement. Thanks to Robin also, for help in pulling the book together. Thanks to Jill Grinberg for being a great agent, a phenomenal reader, and a friend; Dawn Seferian at Counterpoint for pitch-perfect editing that saved me from myself more than once; and Stephanie Hoppe for her smart copyediting. Also thanks to Trish Hoard, John McLeod, Heather McLeod and Keltie Hawkins at Counterpoint, for all their cheer and massive work on behalf of this book.

Some names in the book have been changed; nothing else has, unless through the fault of memory.

Mostly I need to acknowledge that my losses have been, one and all, filled in with much greater graces. This is not so for everyone. For those whose losses have been large and unfillable, such as the parents of sick children, my acknowledgements go to you. Many of you have used your pain to make the world a safer place for all of us.

On the note of grace, my gratitude and my love flow always to the Two Gorgeous Guys.